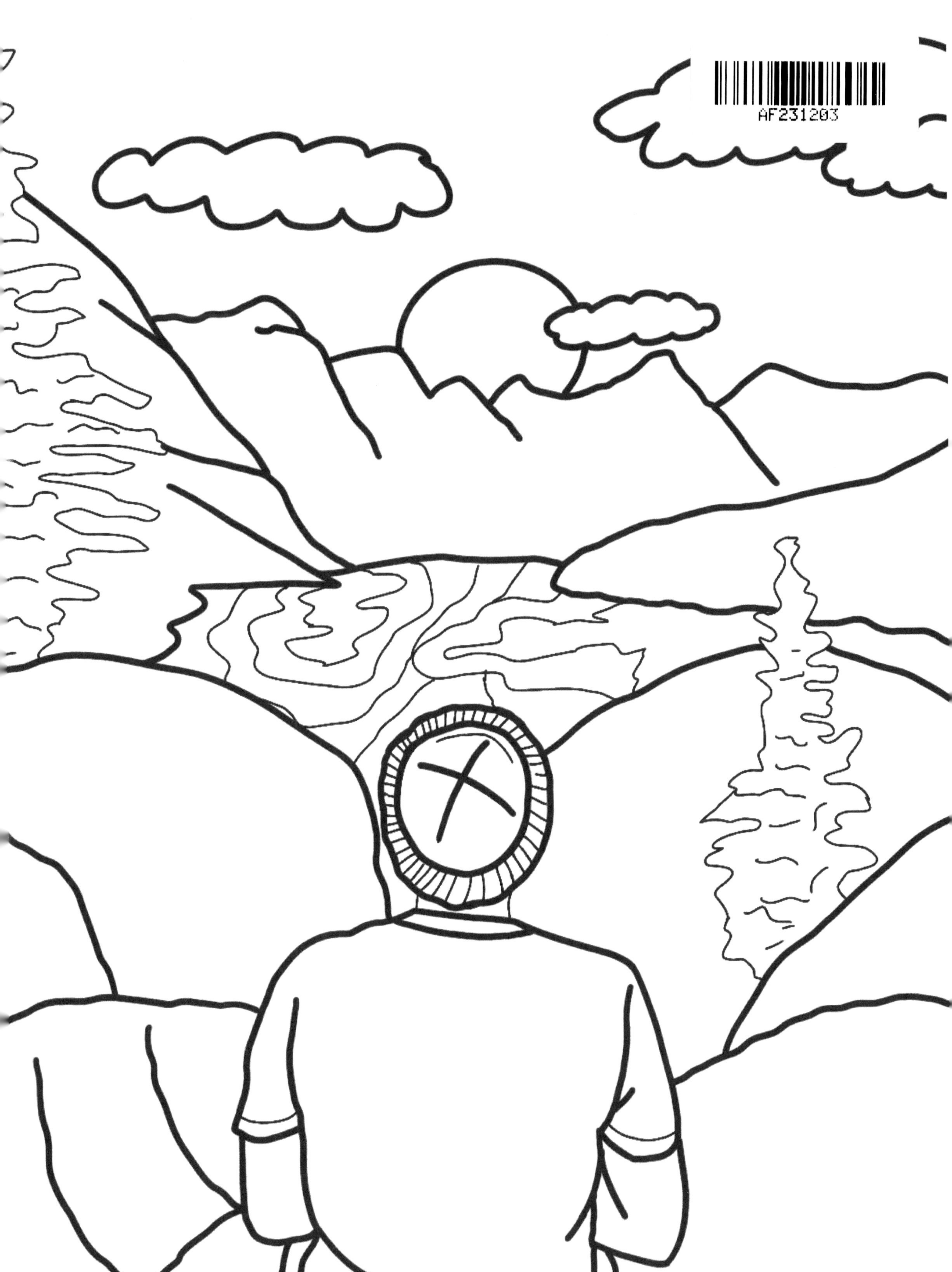
AF231203

Published by
Revolutionary Hearts Industries
Illustrated by Naomi Winston

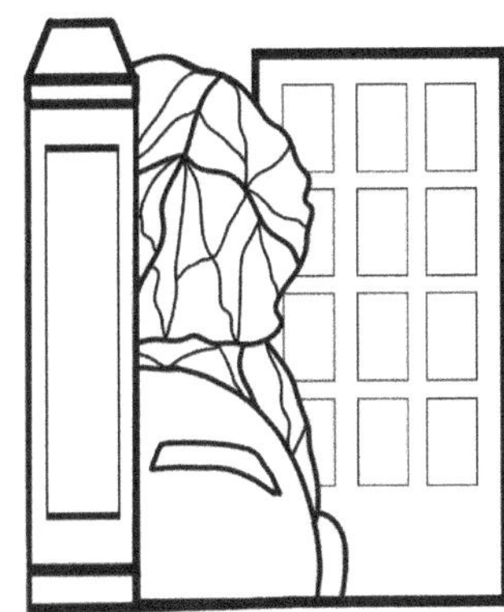

To a world adventurer,

The world is such a HUGE place, and although we can read, watch videos, and scroll on social media to see what others are doing outdoors, take the adventure for yourself!

There are so many options on how to soak up some sun today, which can be overwhelming. Here are some options on how you can get outside! Remember that even when it is hard to make friends, trying new hobbies and going to new places can open you up to new possibilities.

Trying new things can be scary, but I live by the phrase: "I would rather move through my fear than let it stop me from experiencing incredible memories." Don't let your fear or self-doubt keep you from meeting your next best friend, finding your favorite sport, or making a memory that will last a lifetime.

I have complete faith in you, so all you have to do is to believe in yourself. You are capable of a lot more than you think you are!

You are doing amazing, and I cannot wait to see what you do next!

Everything has a purpose, and you are everything!

LETTER FROM THE AUTHOR

ADVENTURE AWAITS OUTSIDE

I won't be afraid of adventure because it could be the best time of my life.

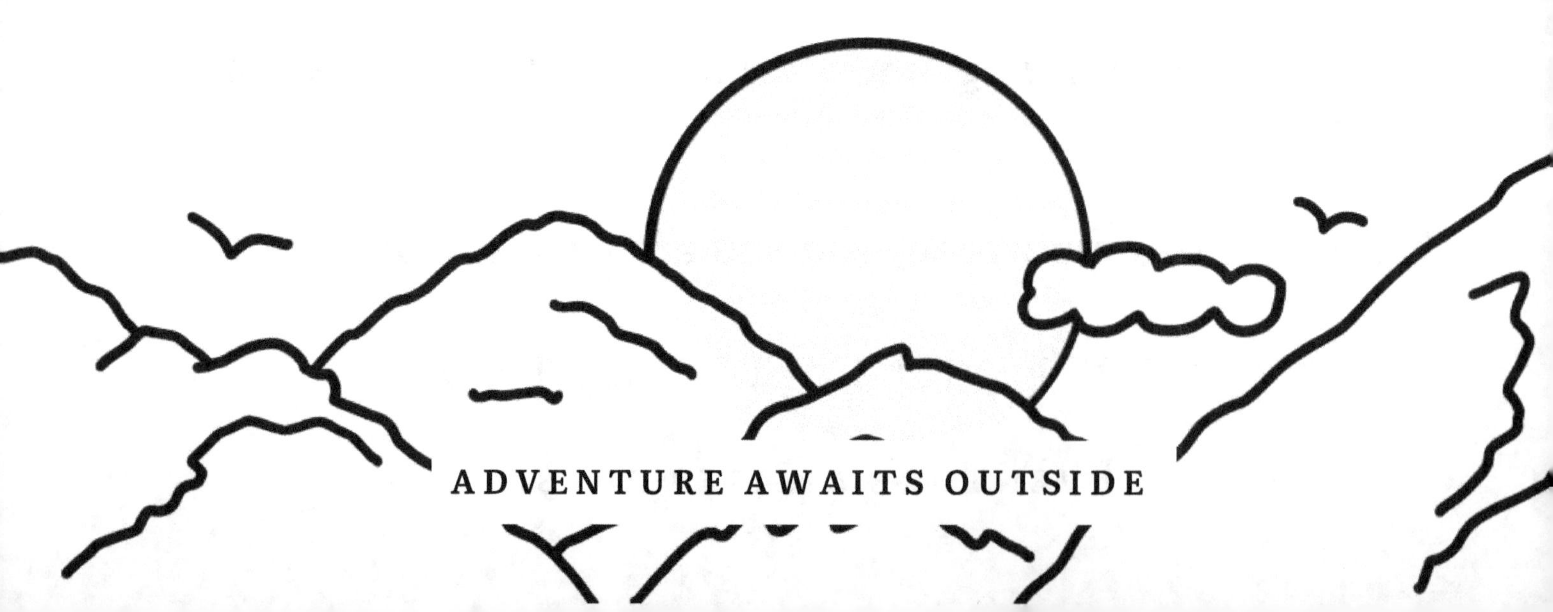

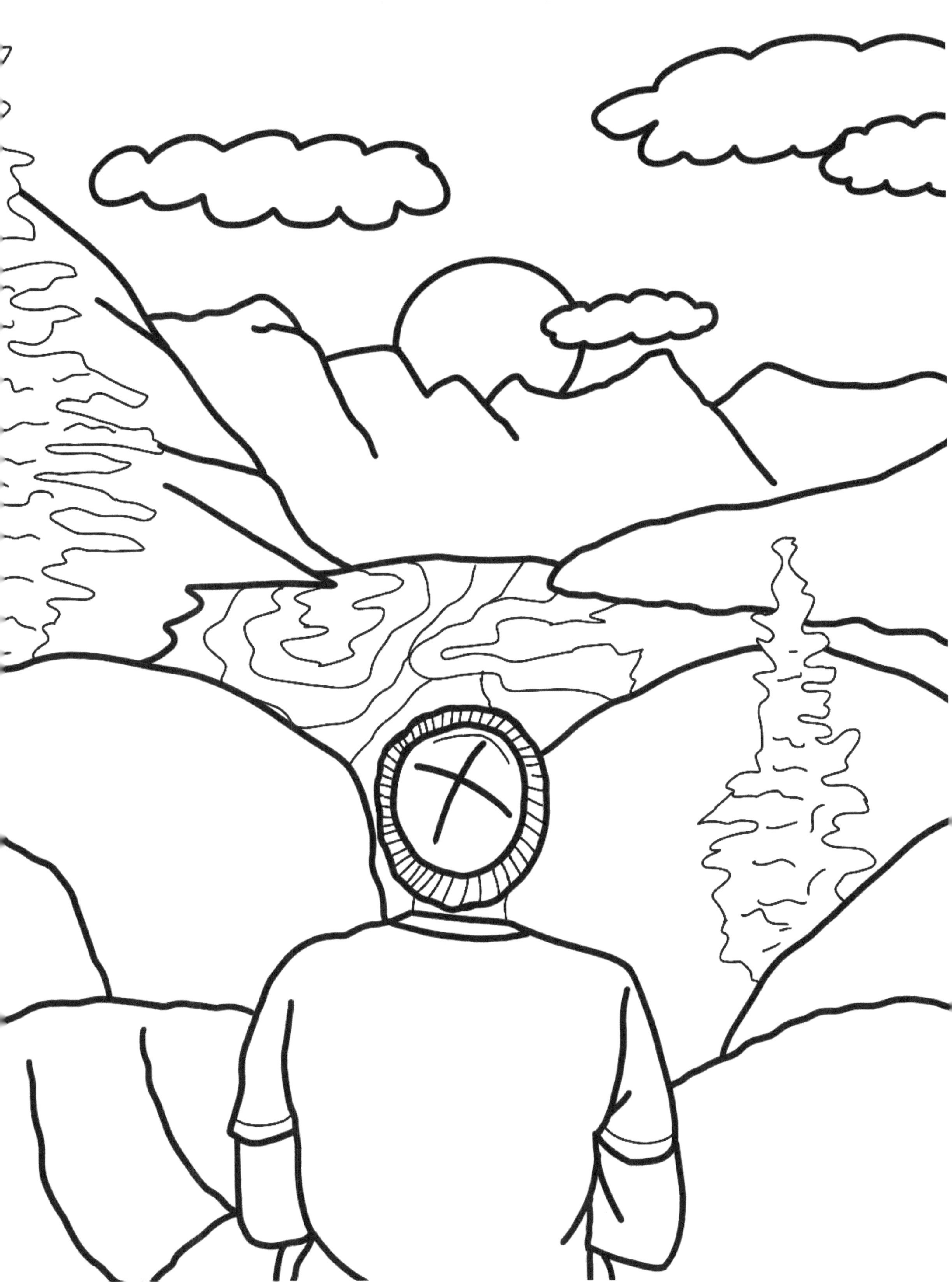

I can take a break from my screens to soak up some sun!

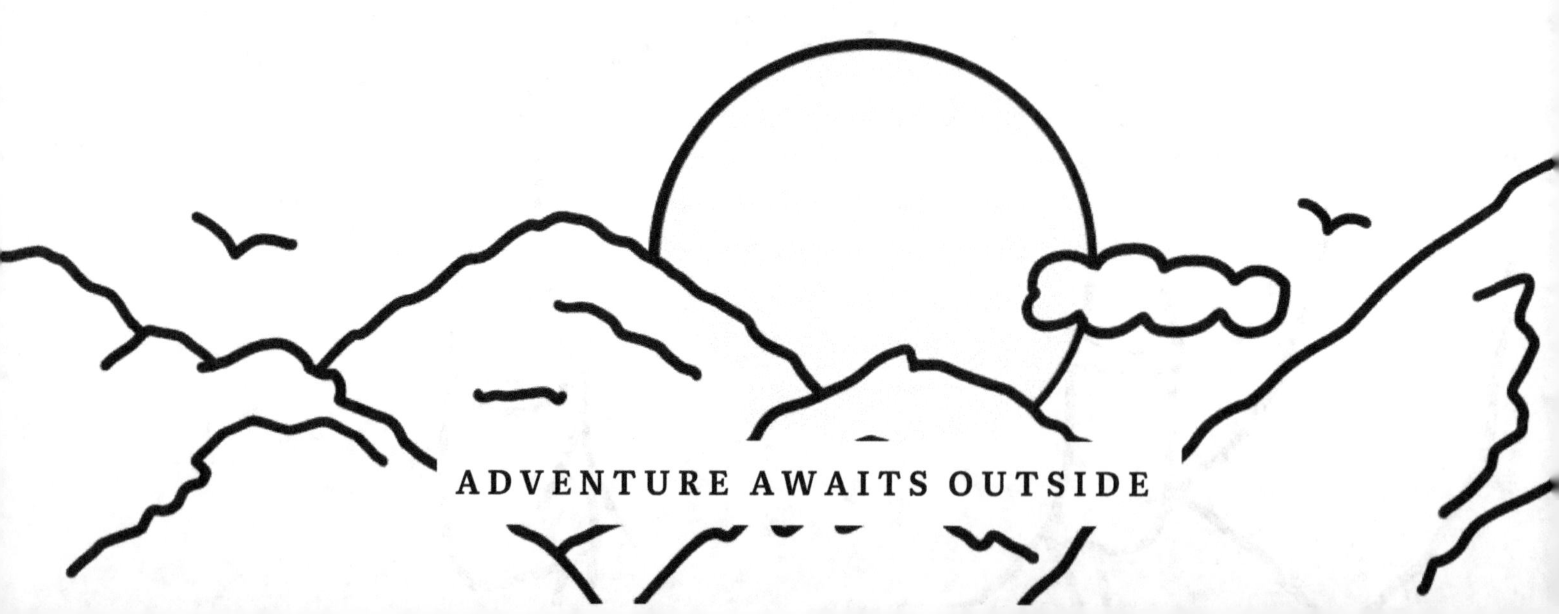

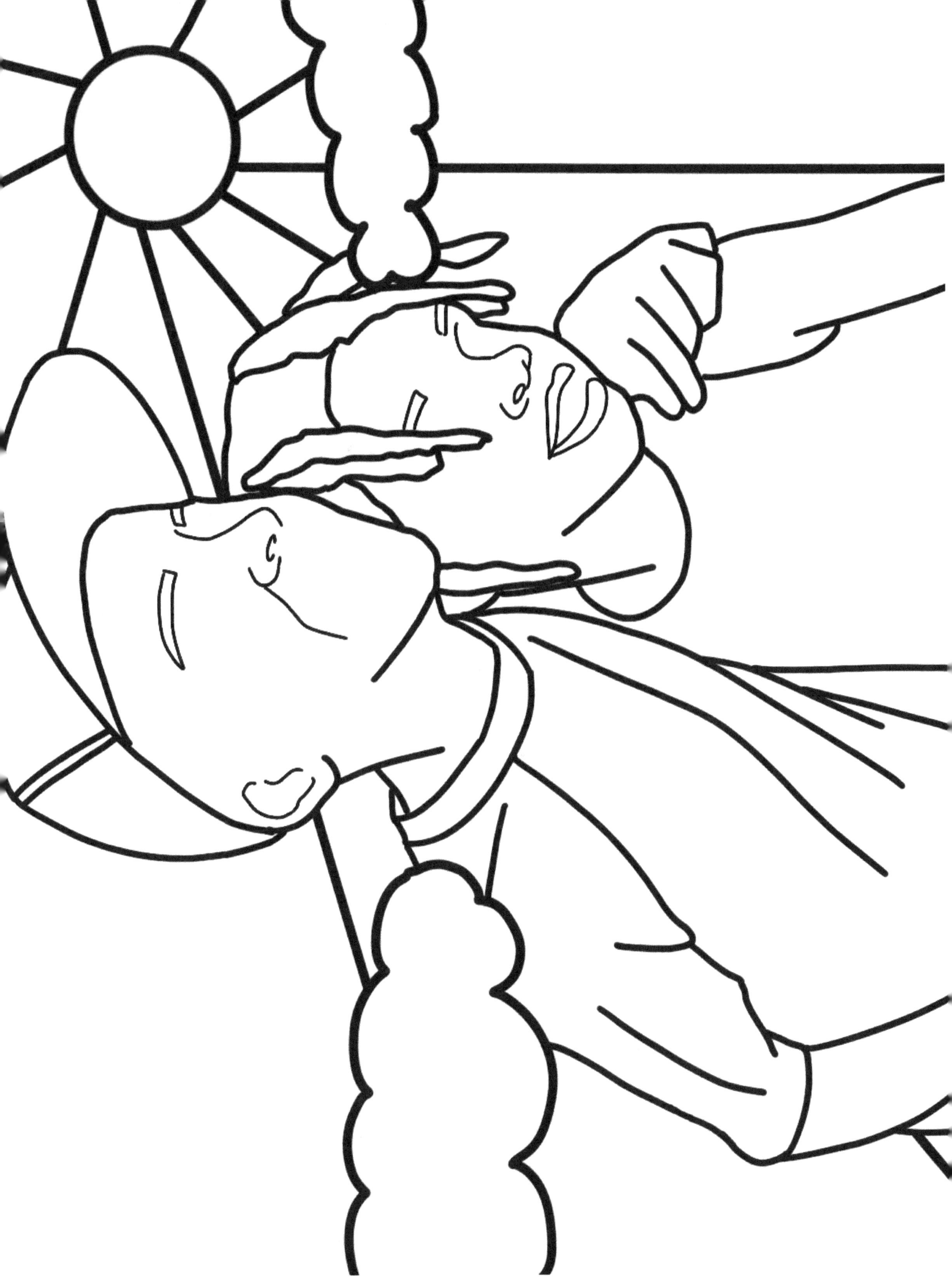

A book is an adventure within itself, and I never know where, who, or when I will end up. I can open a book and start my adventure.

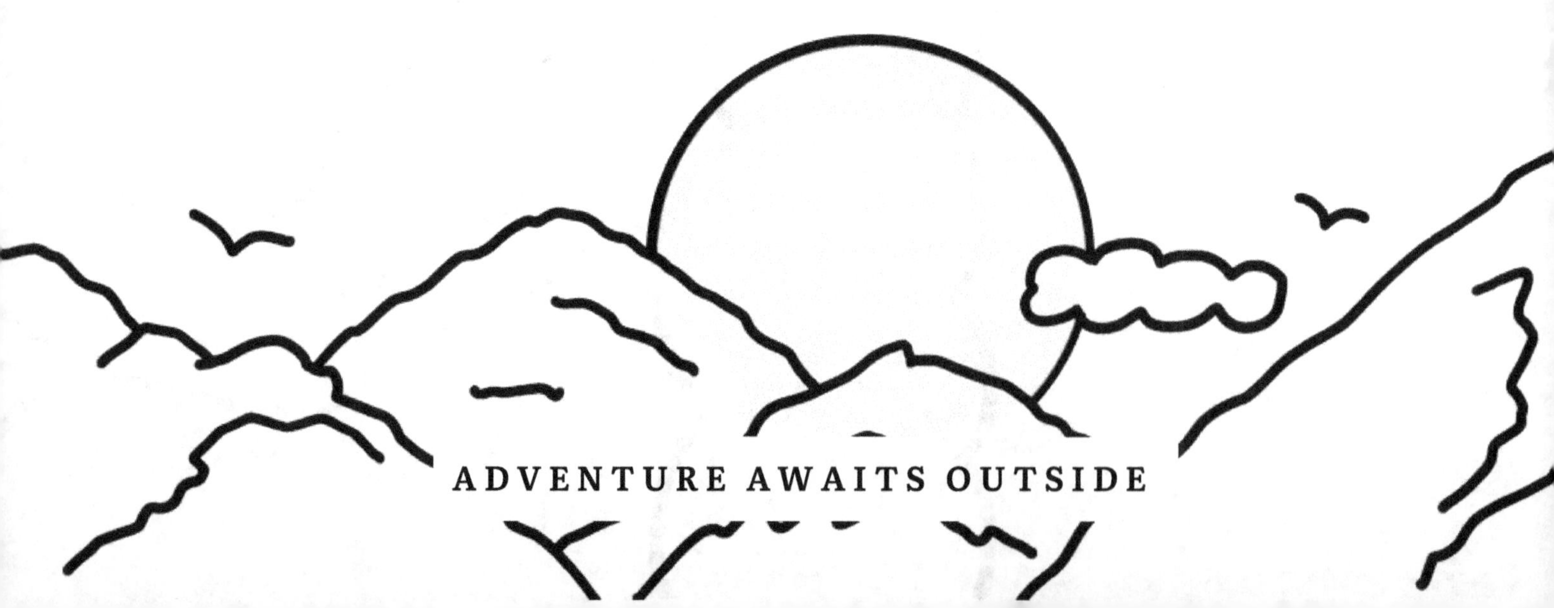

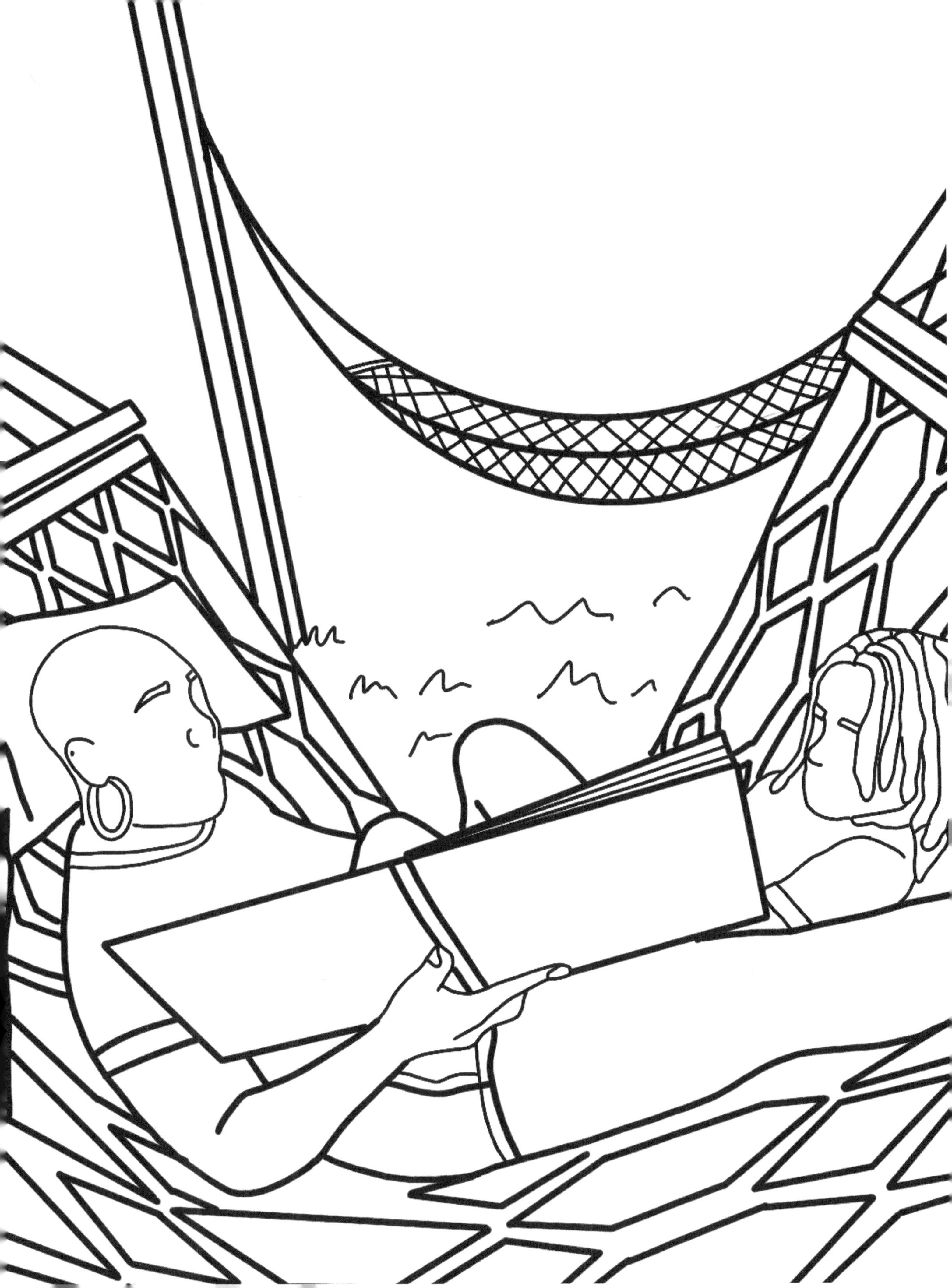

Take a hike (literally). It's good for me!

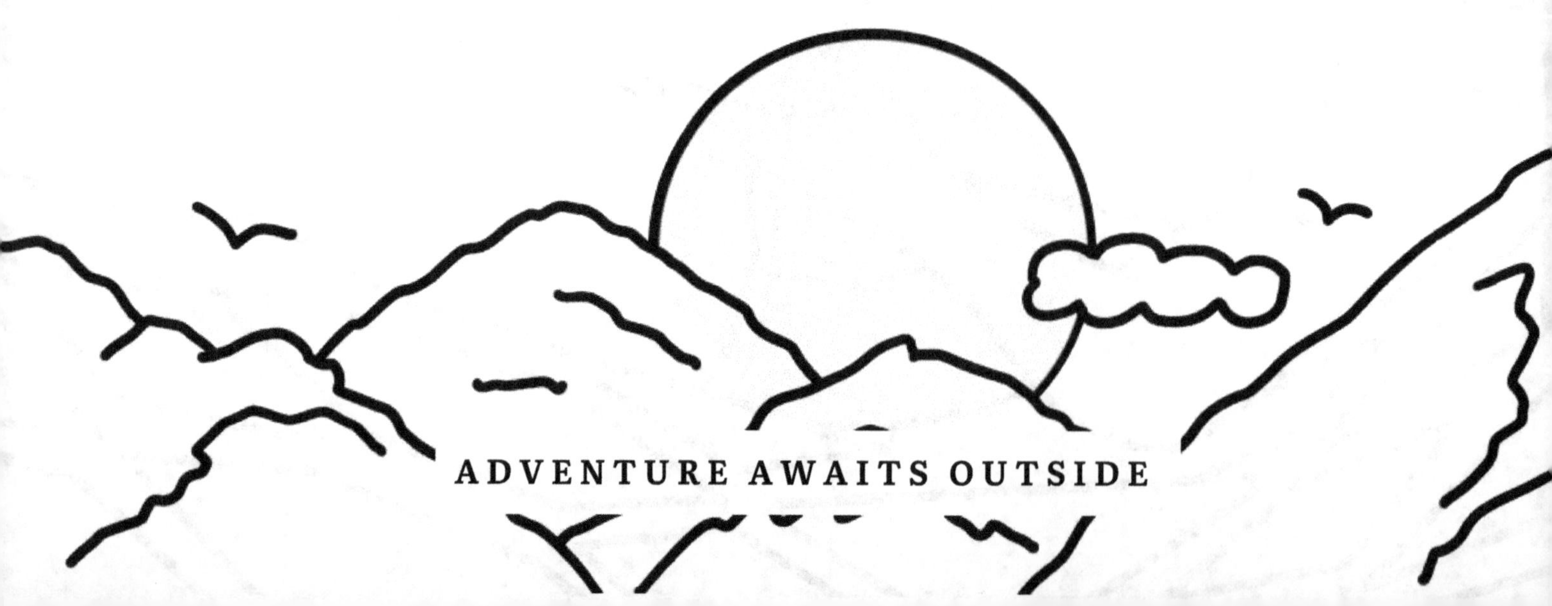

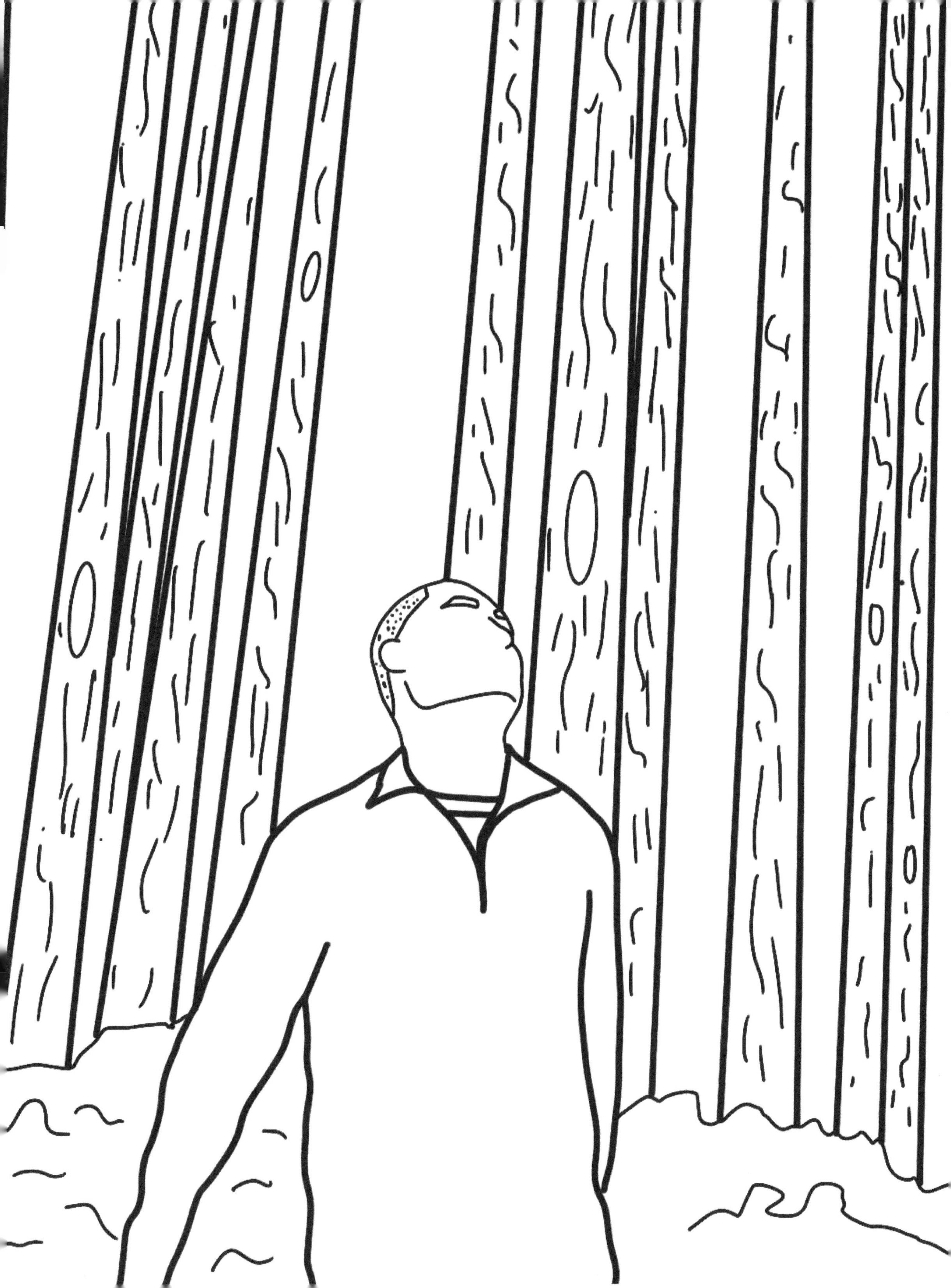

My summer shade is beautiful!

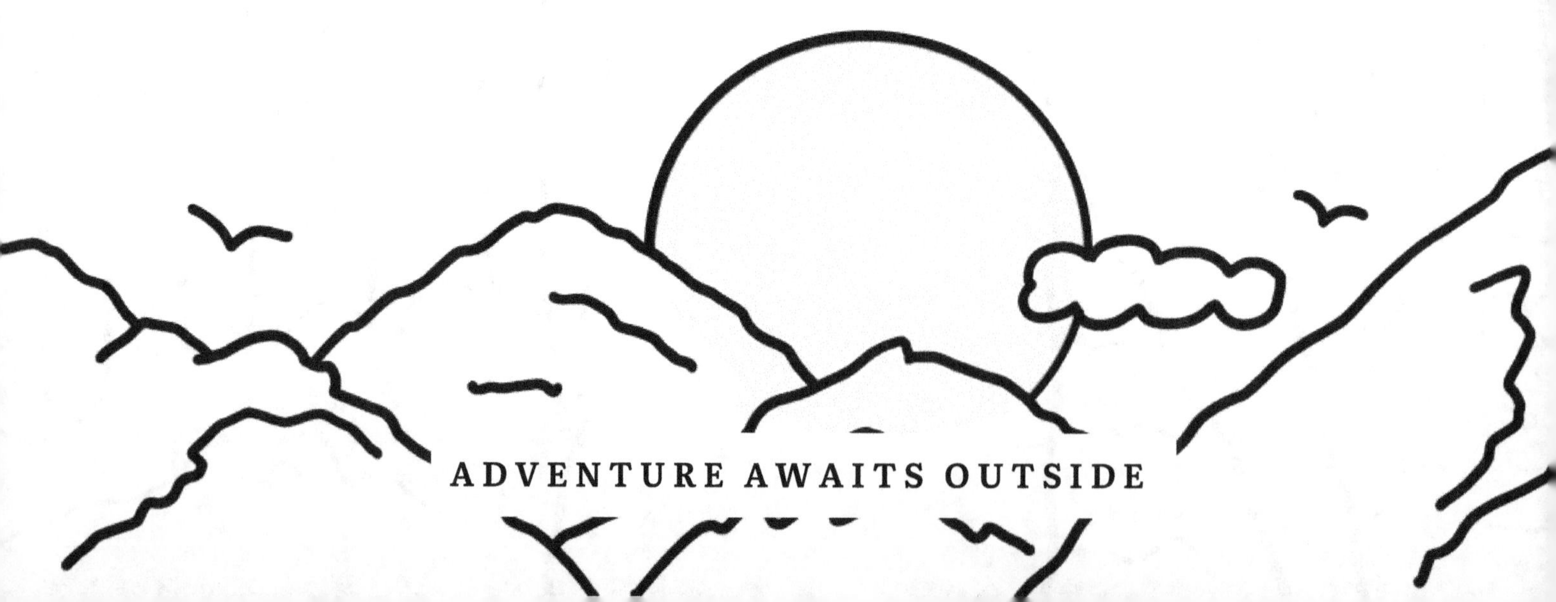

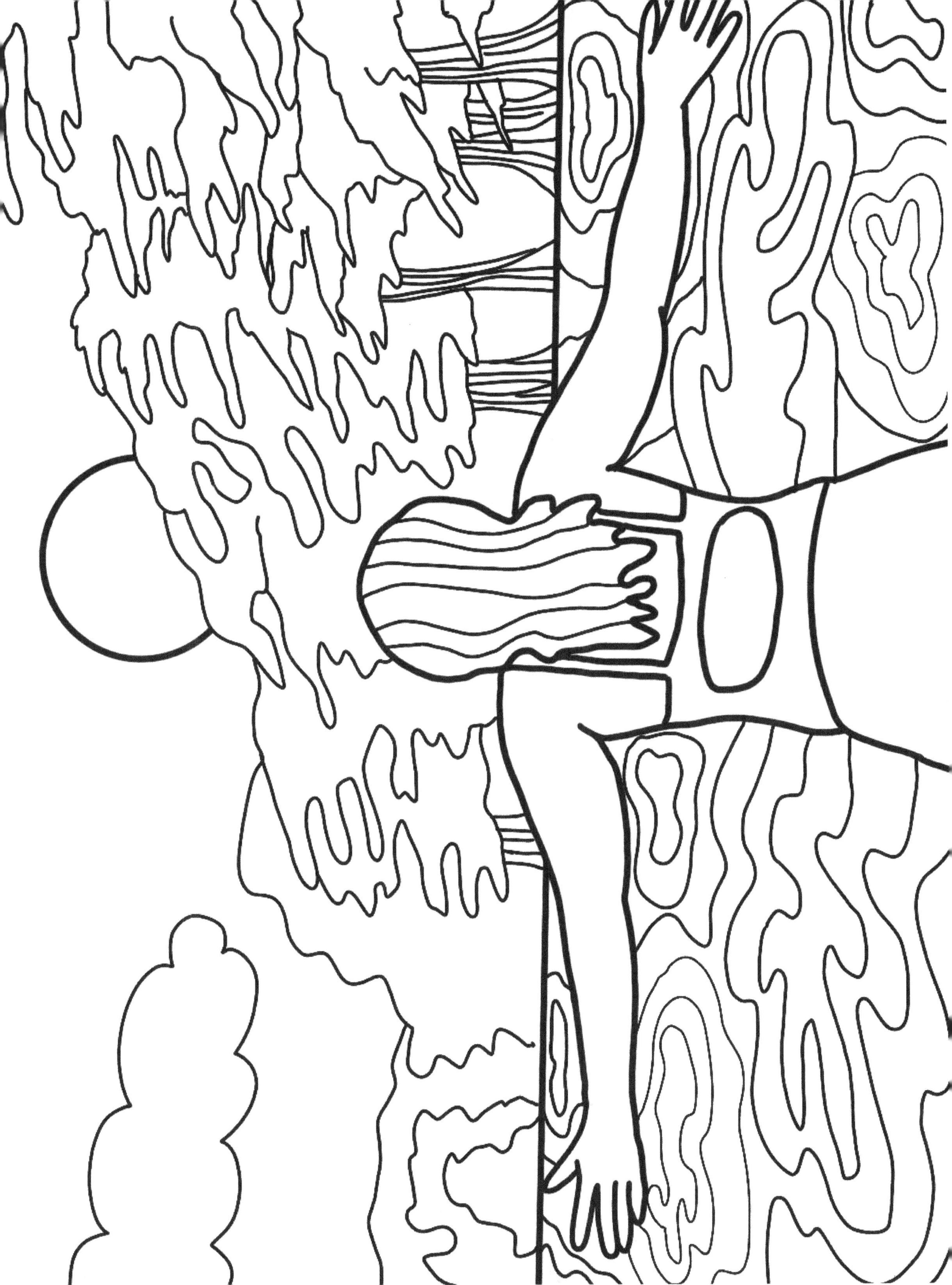

The world isn't as big and scary as I think. I can go out and make friends today!

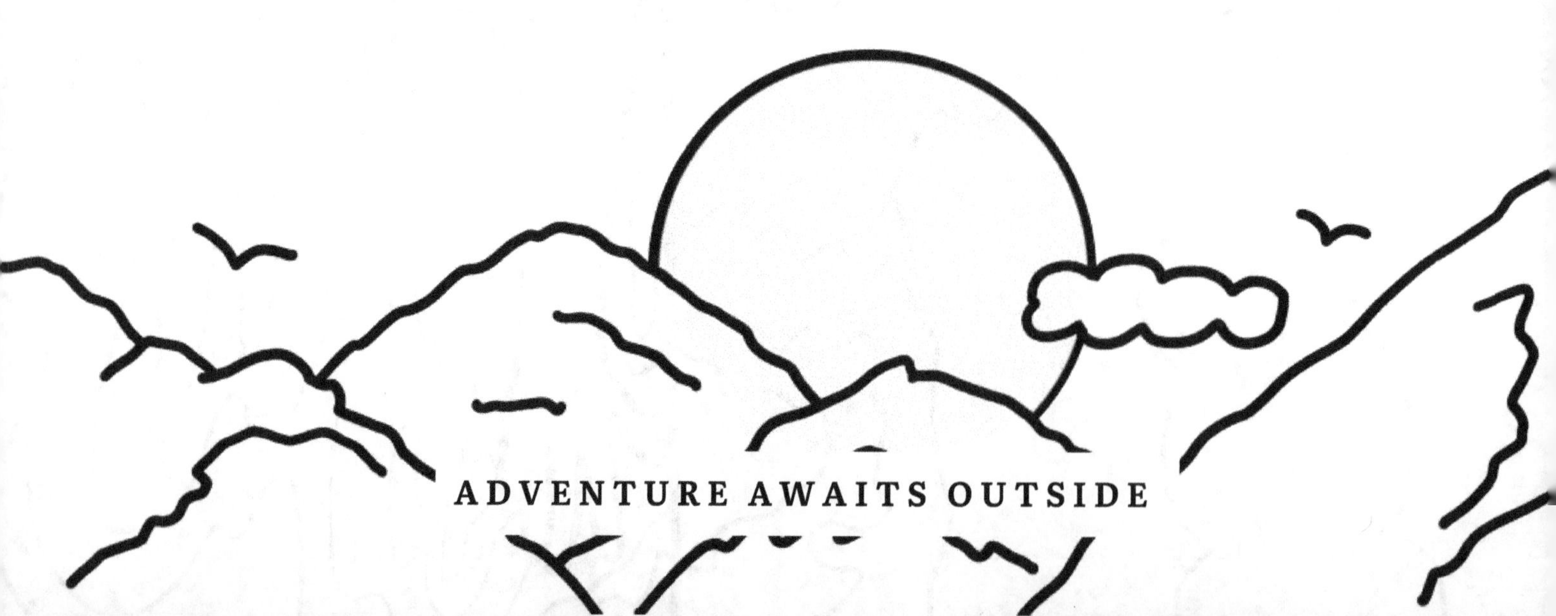

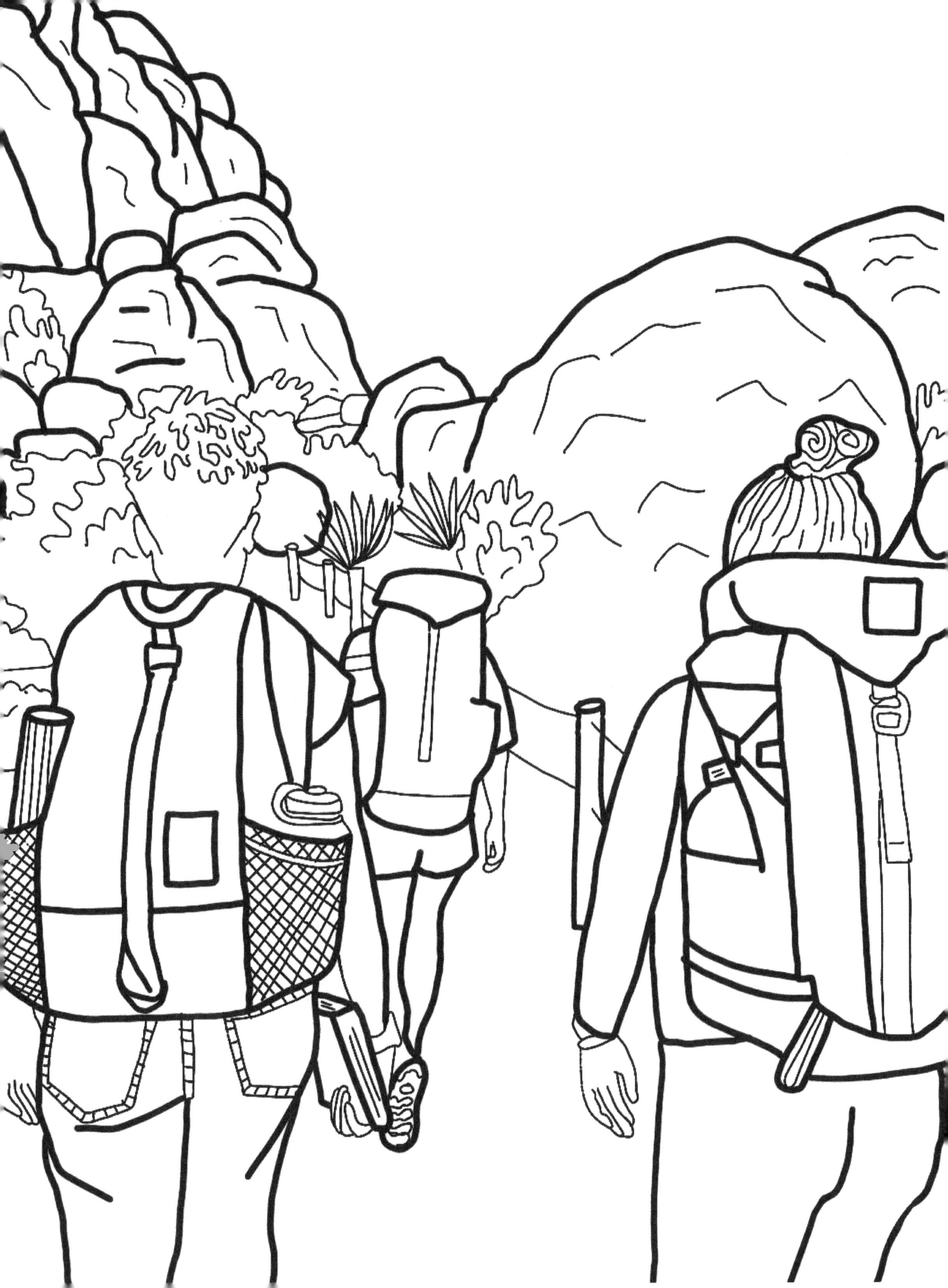

I trust myself, and I trust my body. I know that I can solve hard problems.

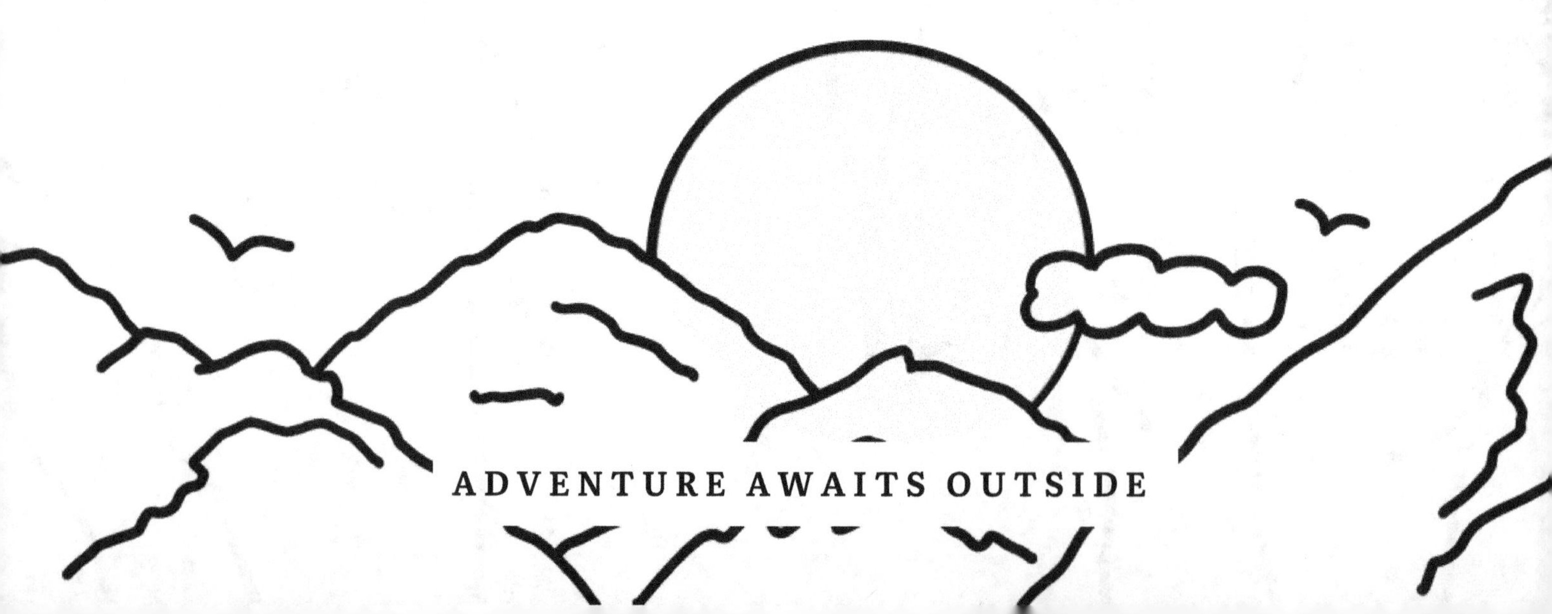

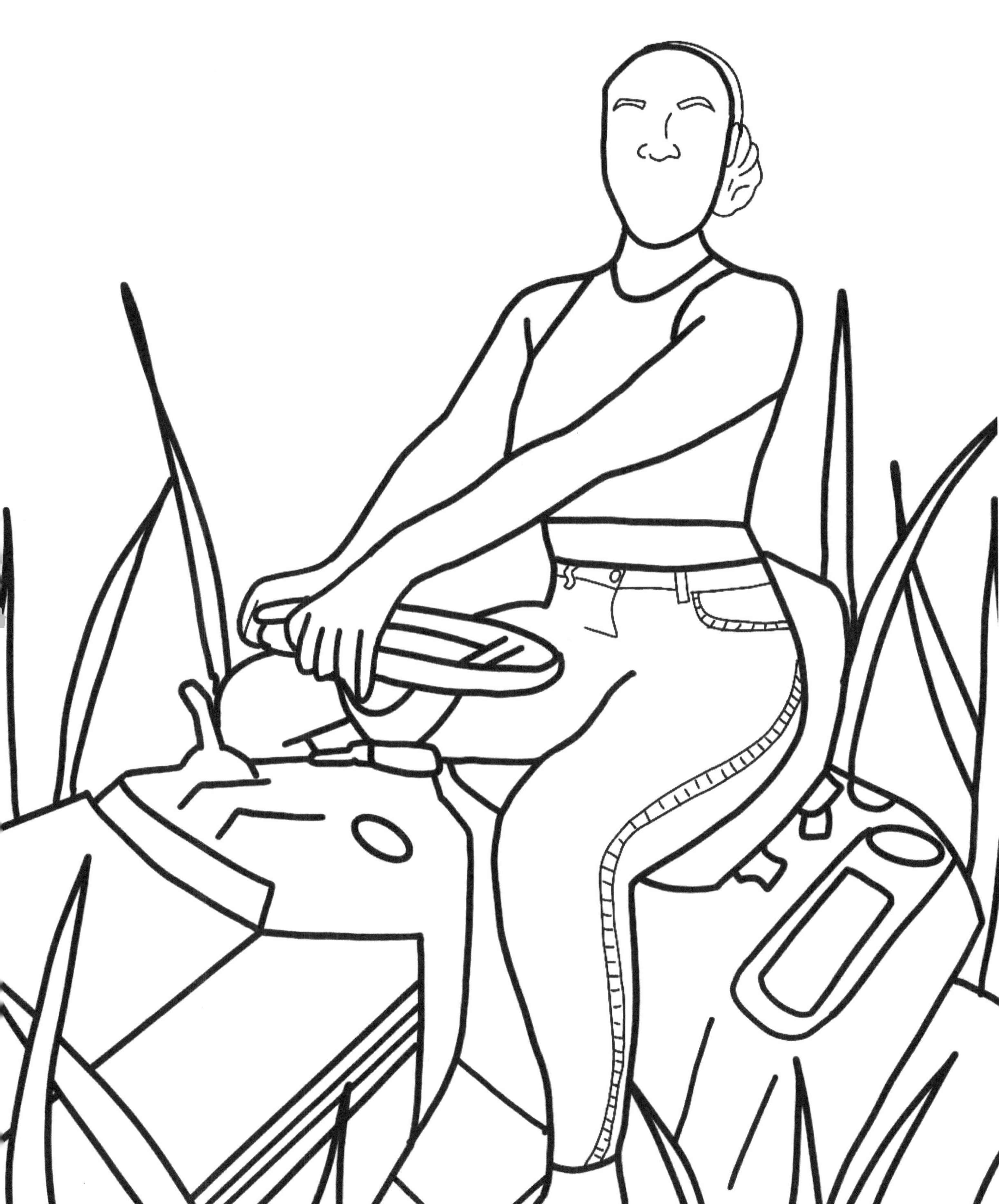

I can reach new heights and know that I am protected to do so.

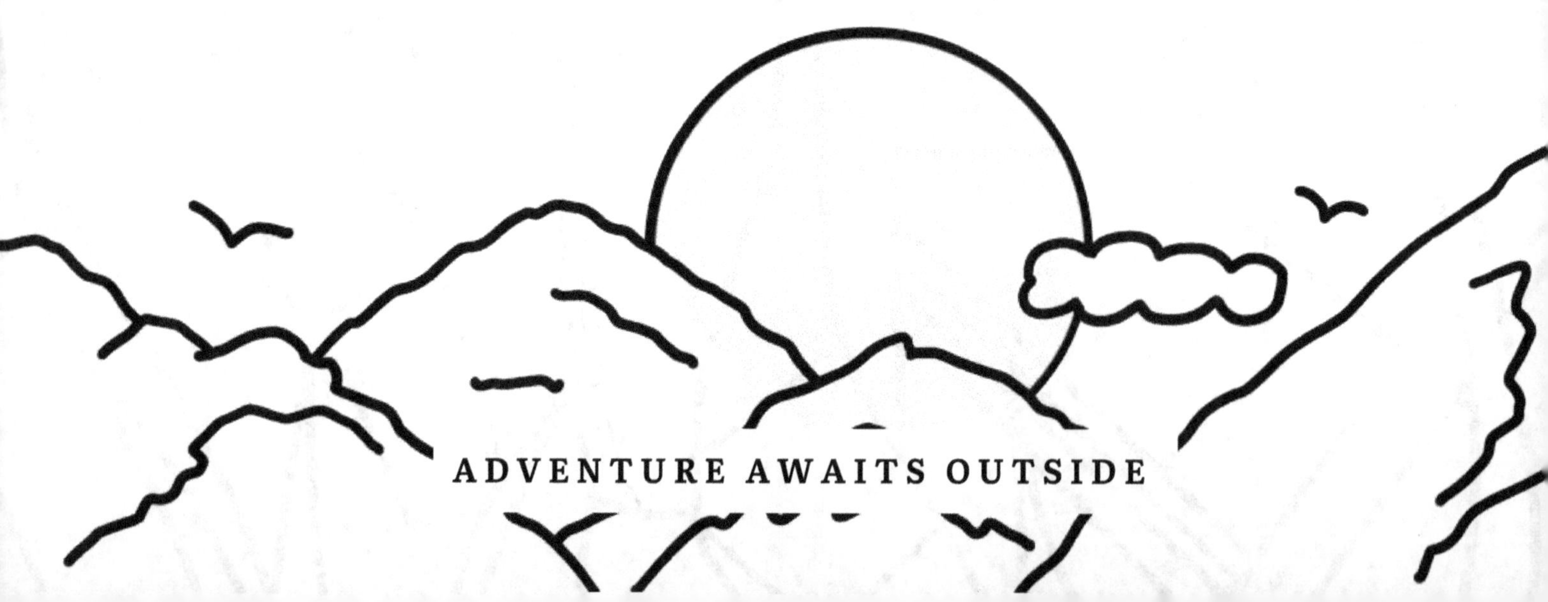

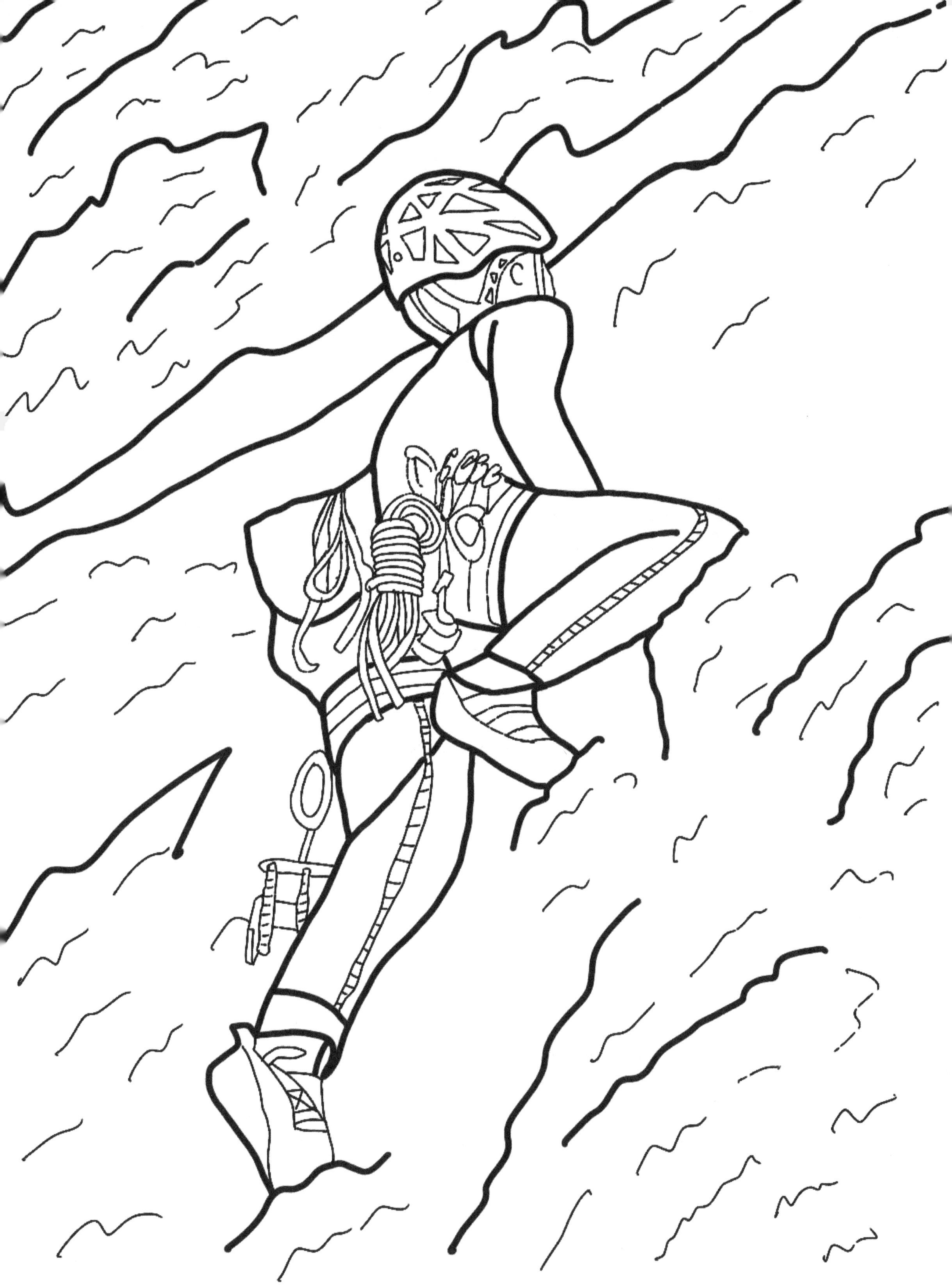

I can create life and grow food to feed myself and others.

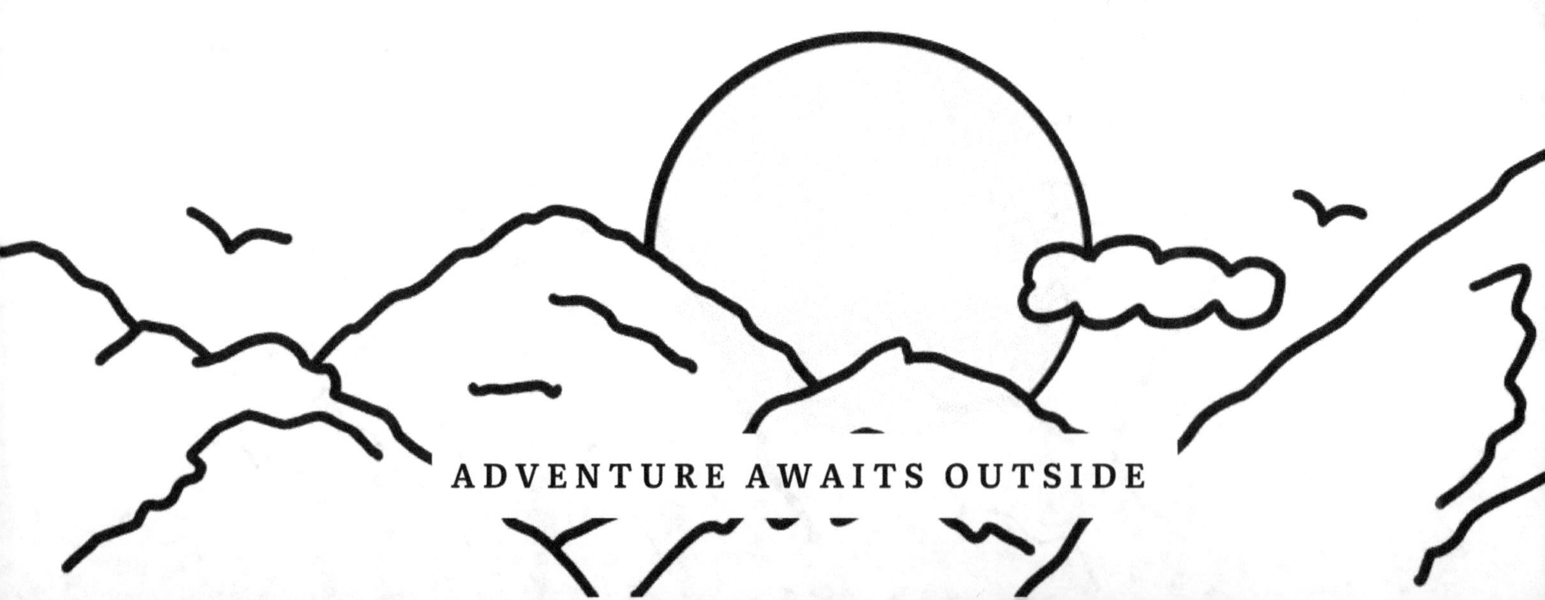

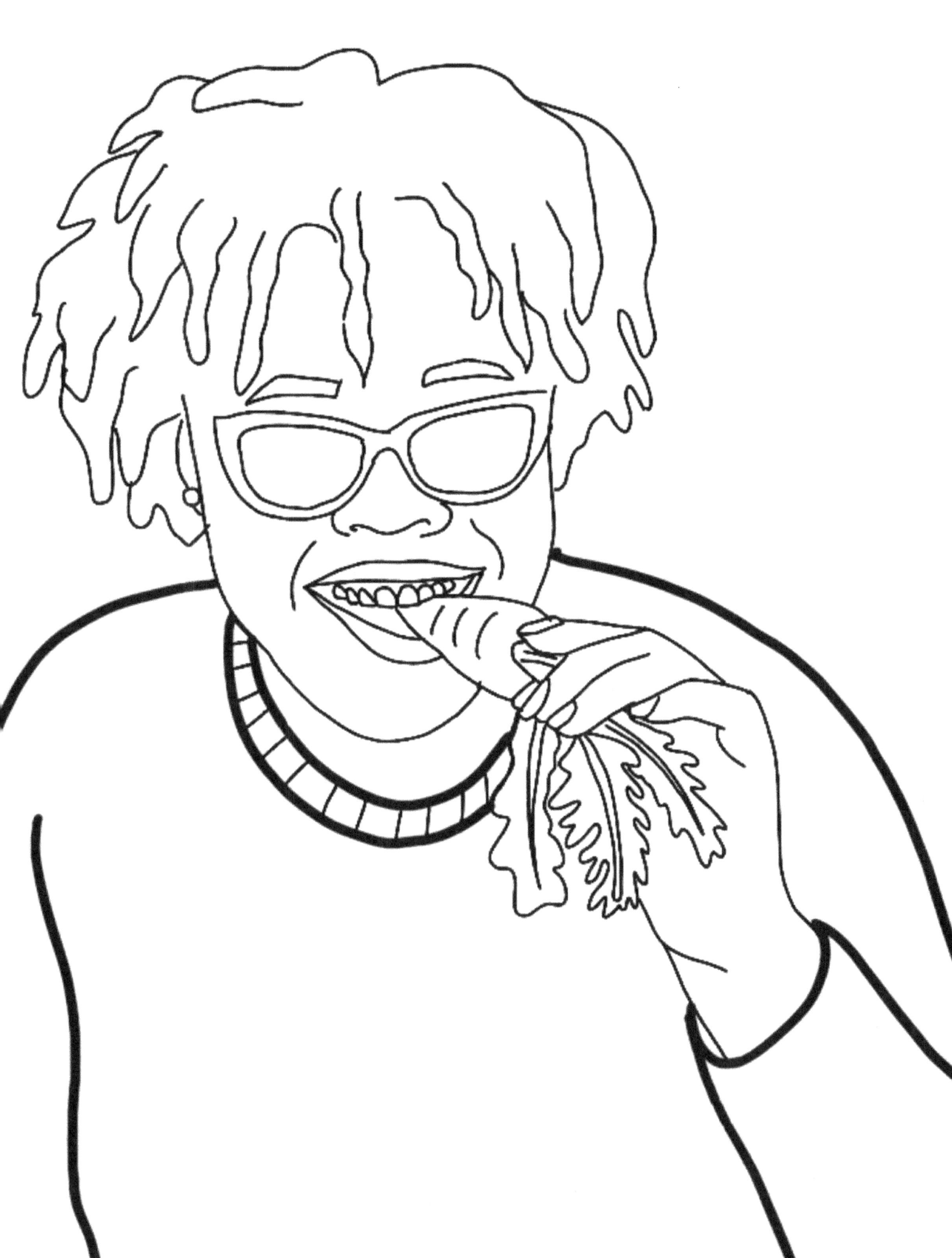

My skin is beautiful just the way that it is.

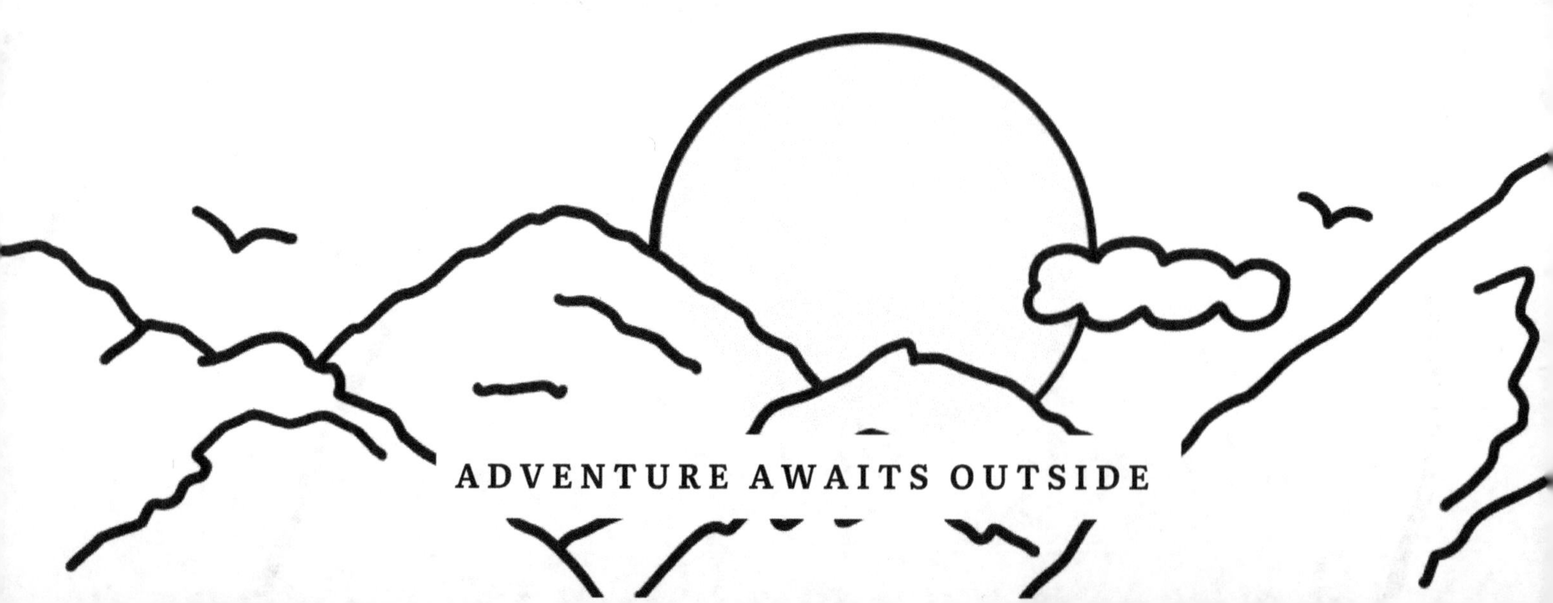

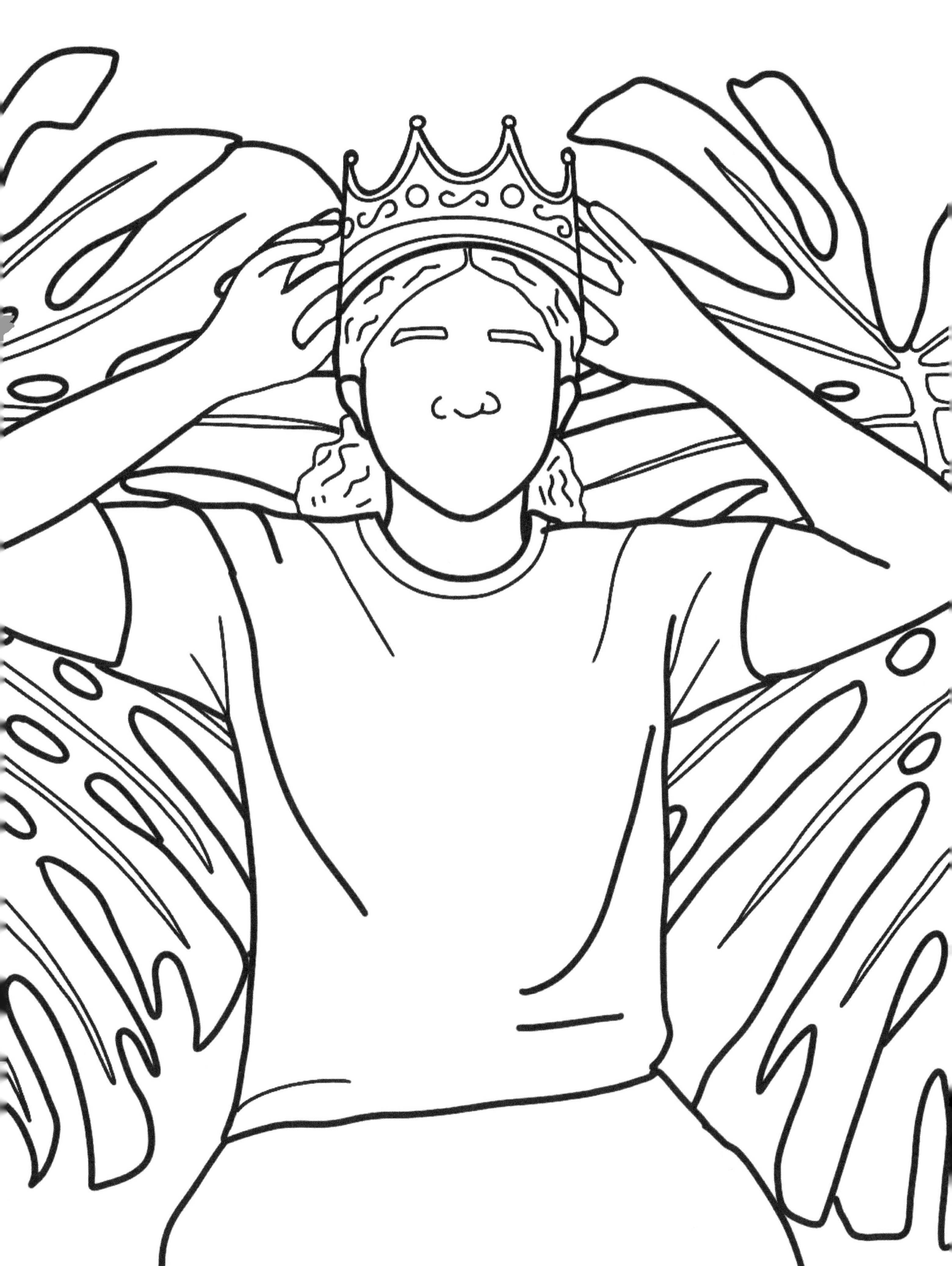

I can spend time with those who matter most to me.

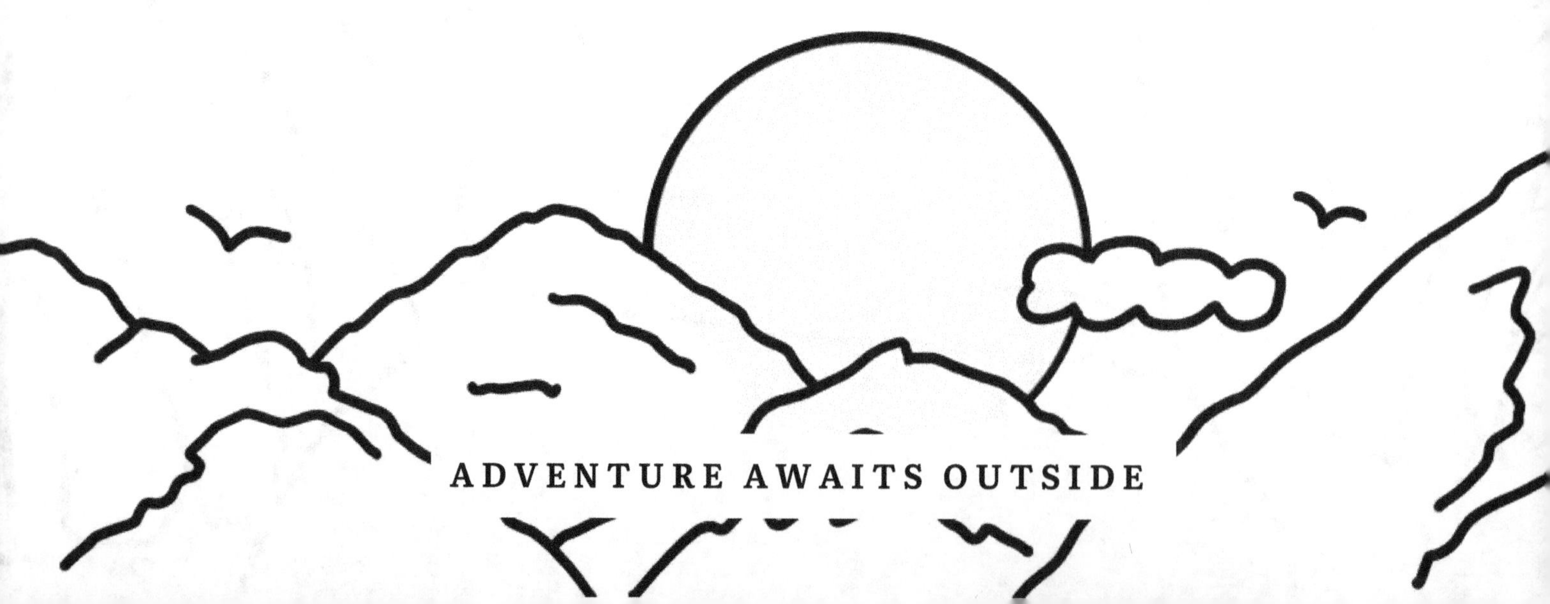

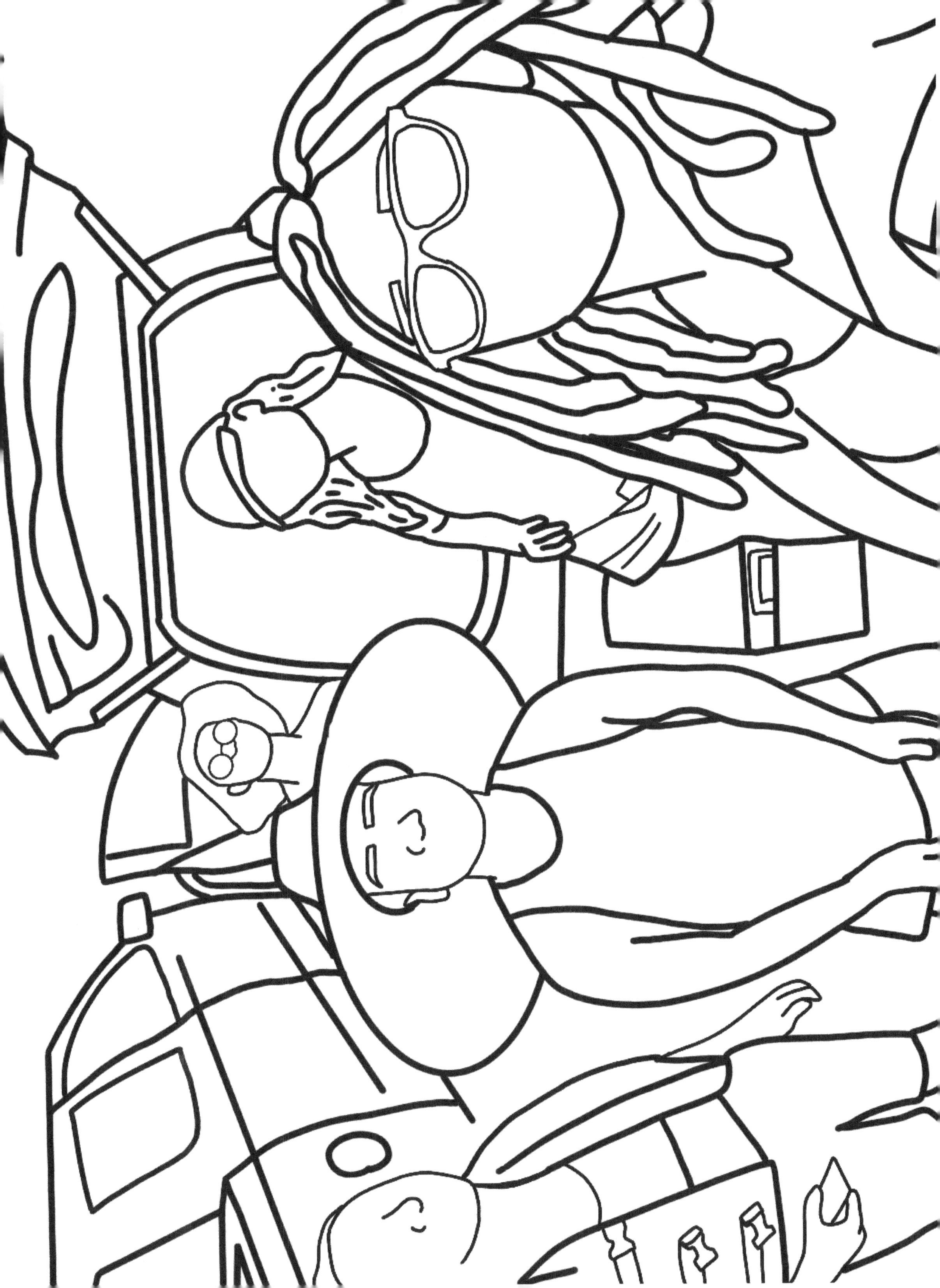

I can remember to wear sunscreen and be safe!

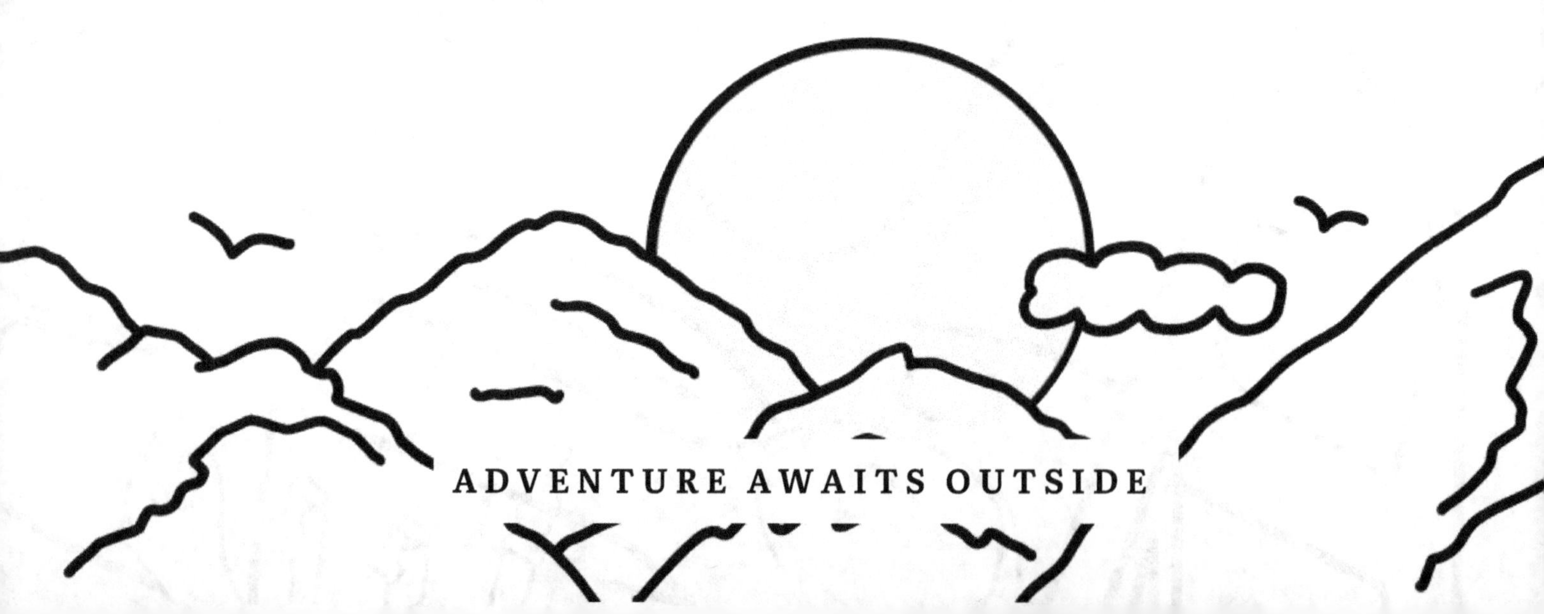

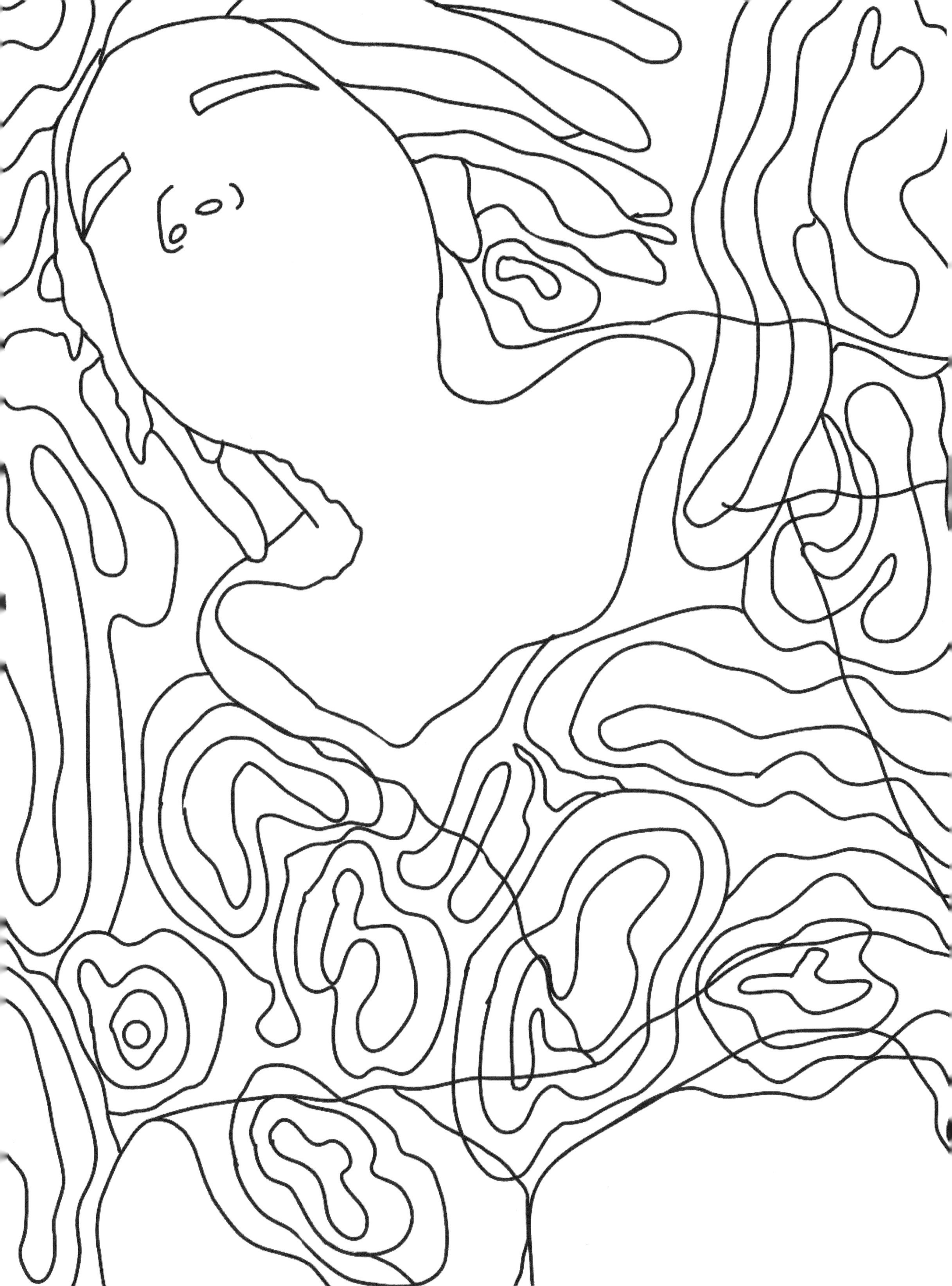

The world is within my reach if I just step outside.

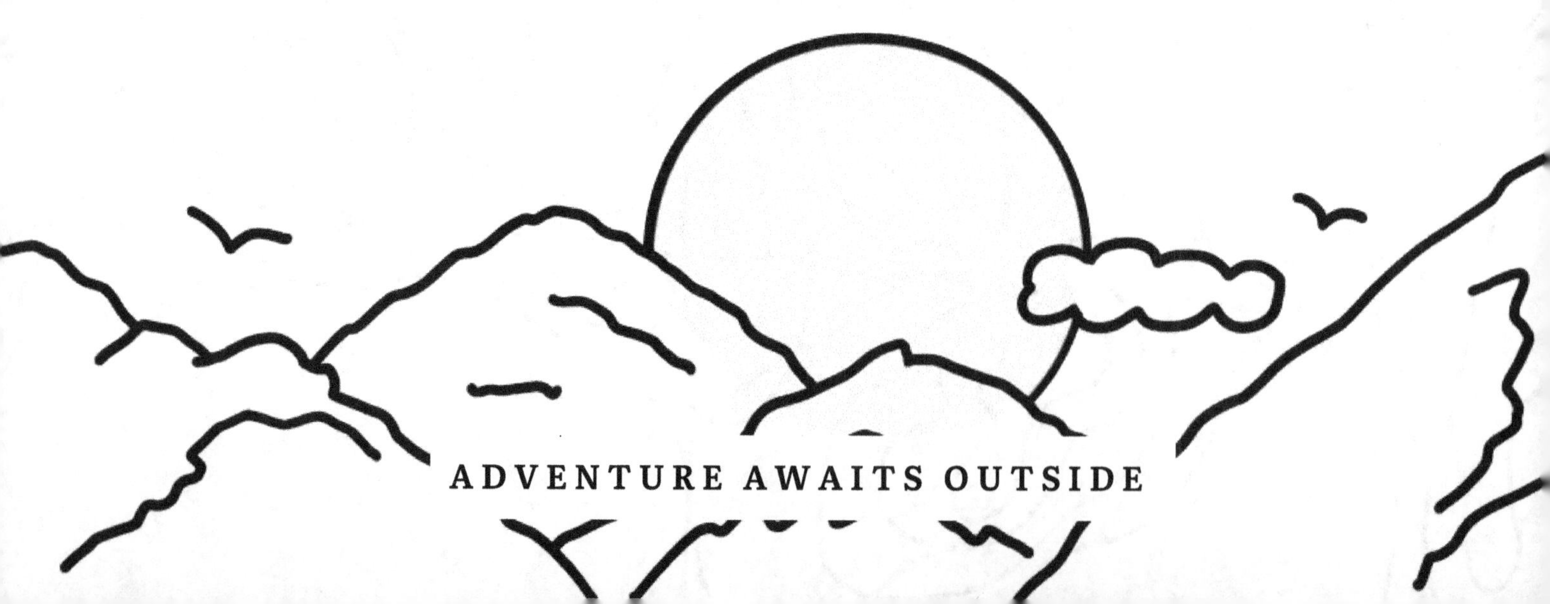

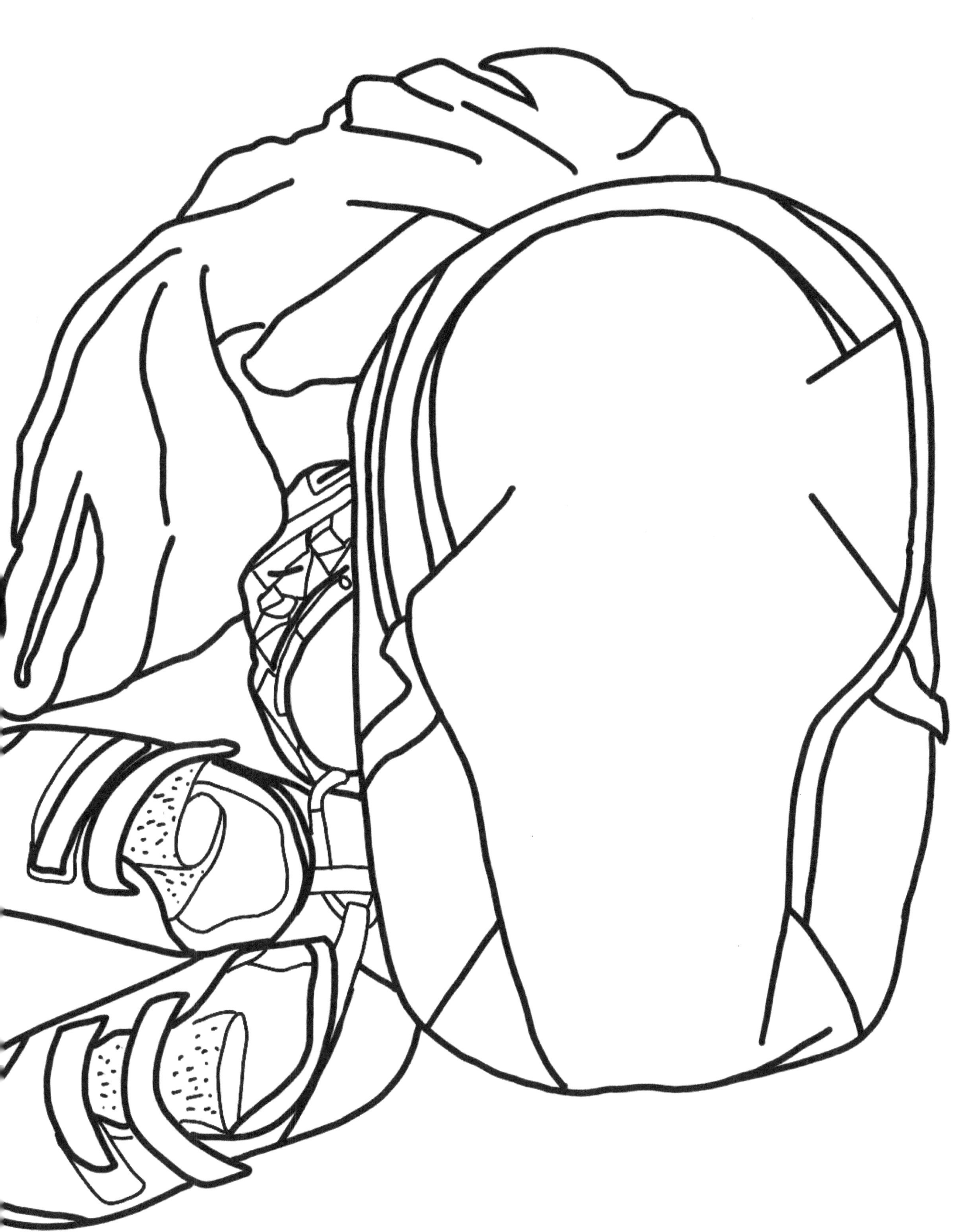

I deserve to be in any space that I want to walk into.

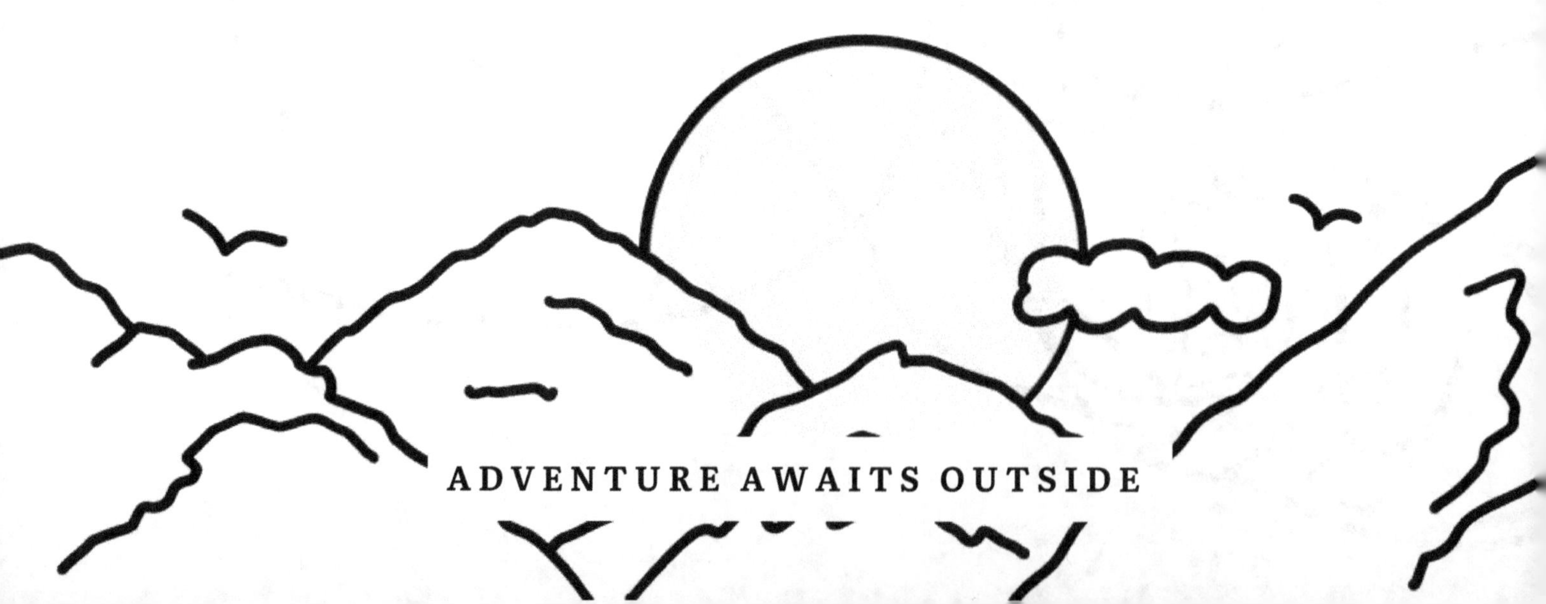

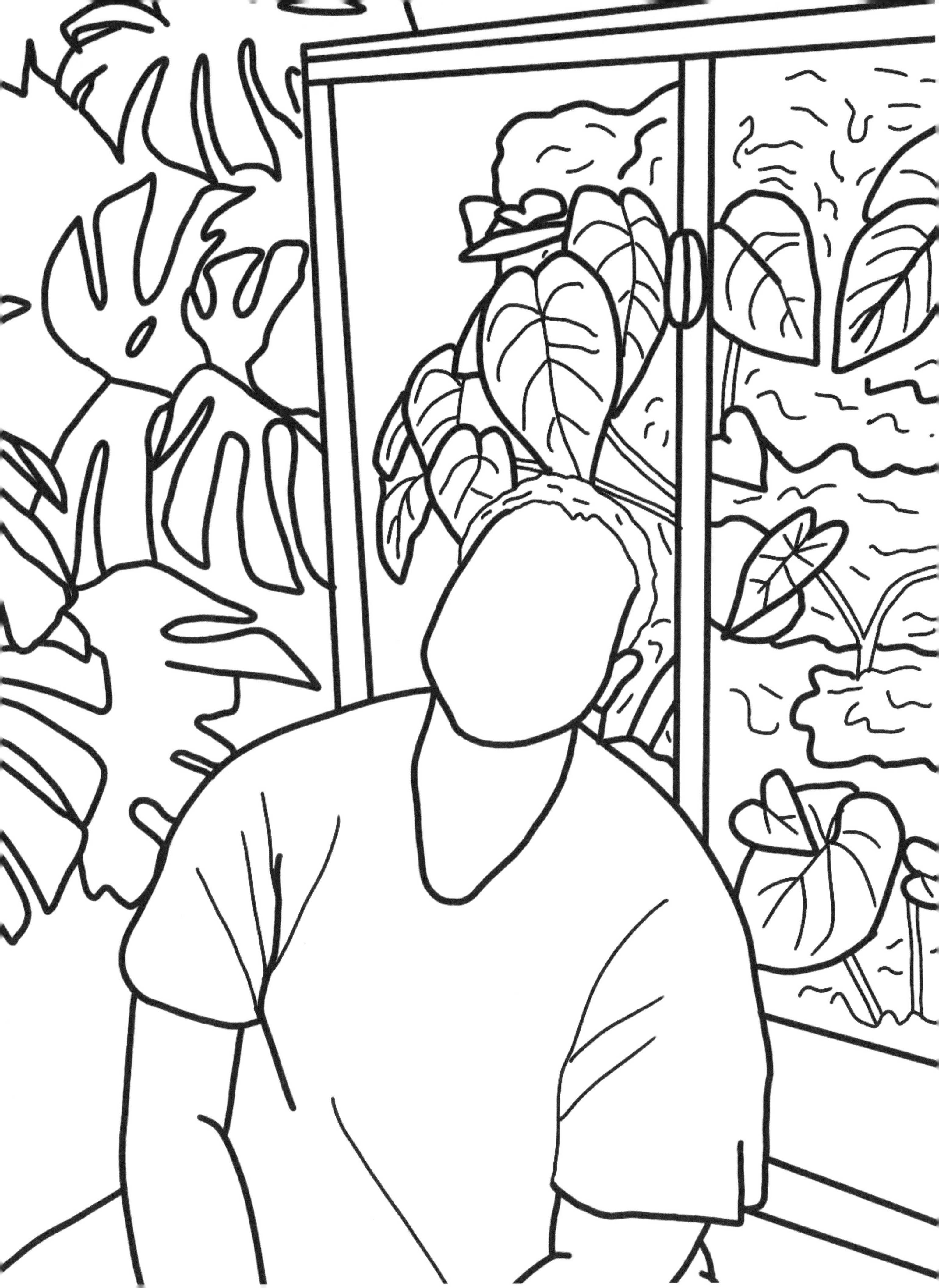

I belong.

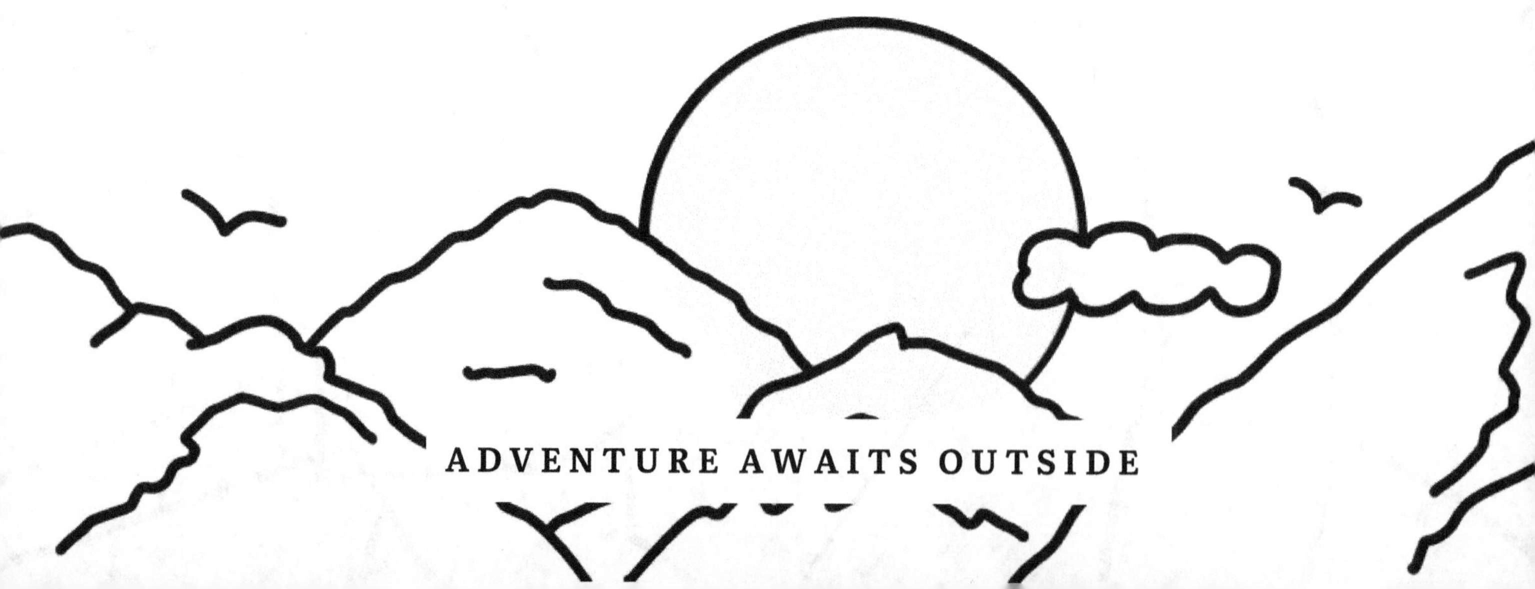

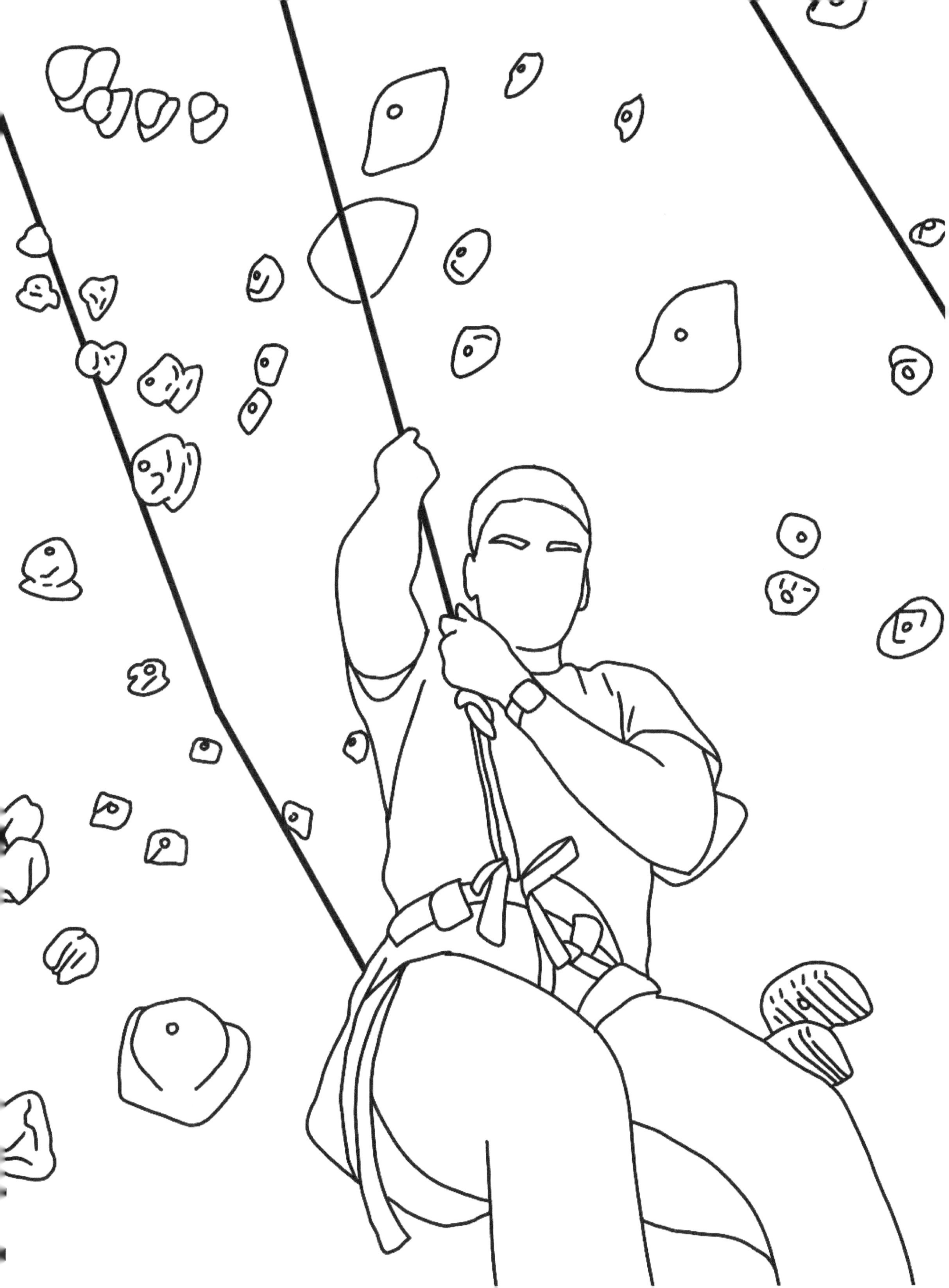

I deserve to enjoy the summer!

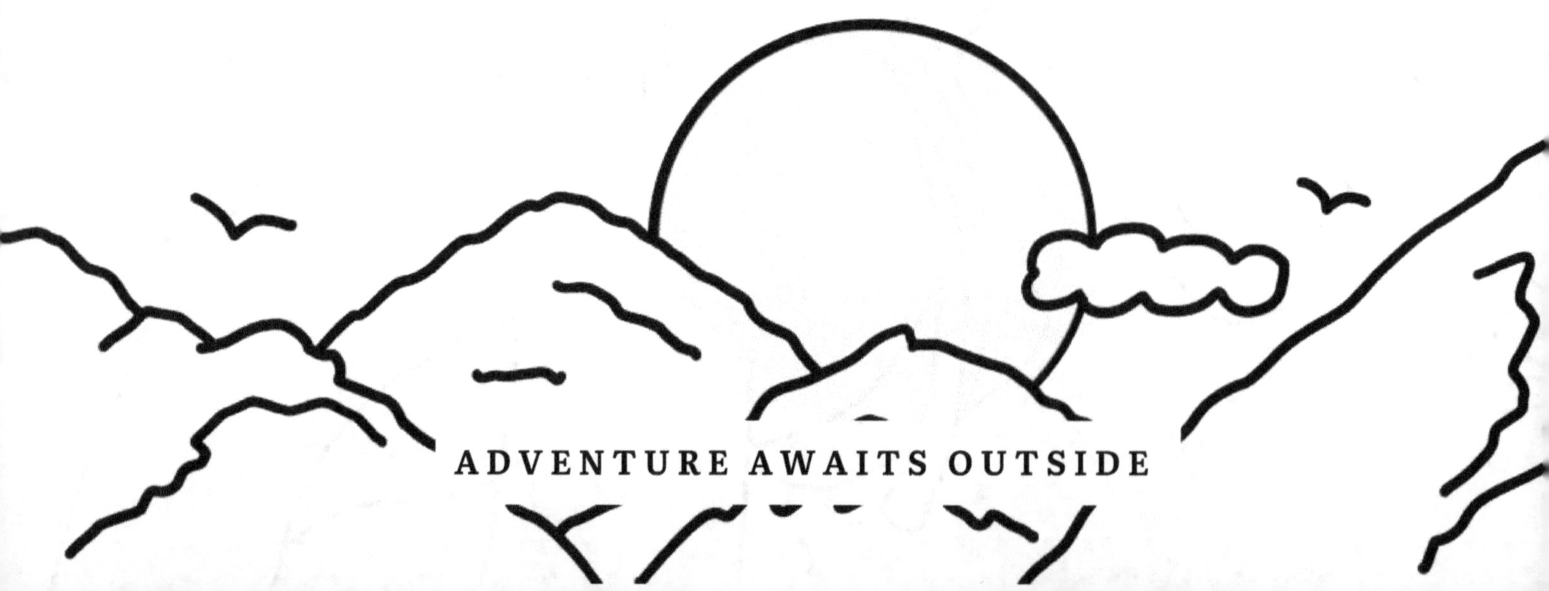

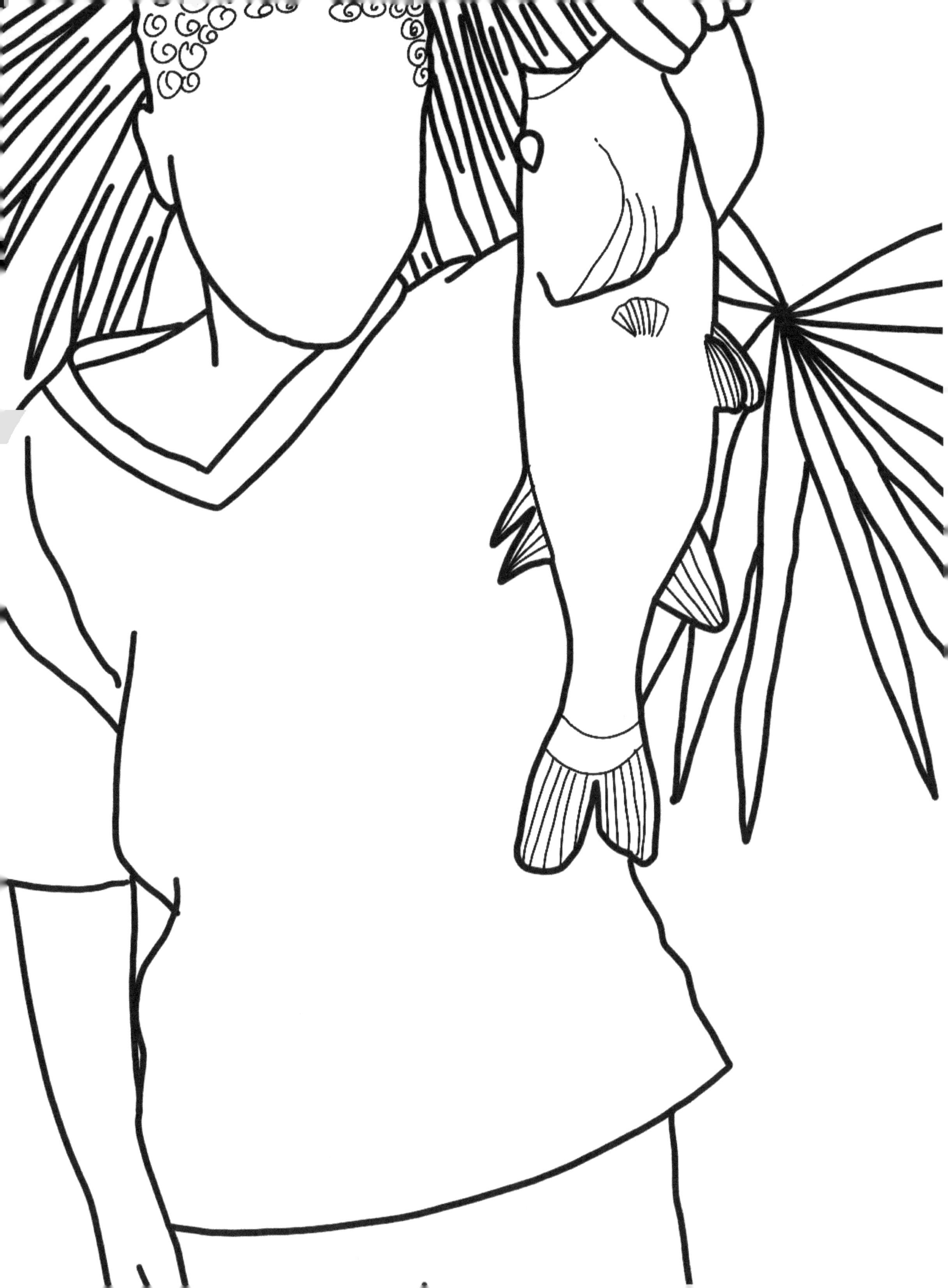

The sun loves me, and I love the sun!

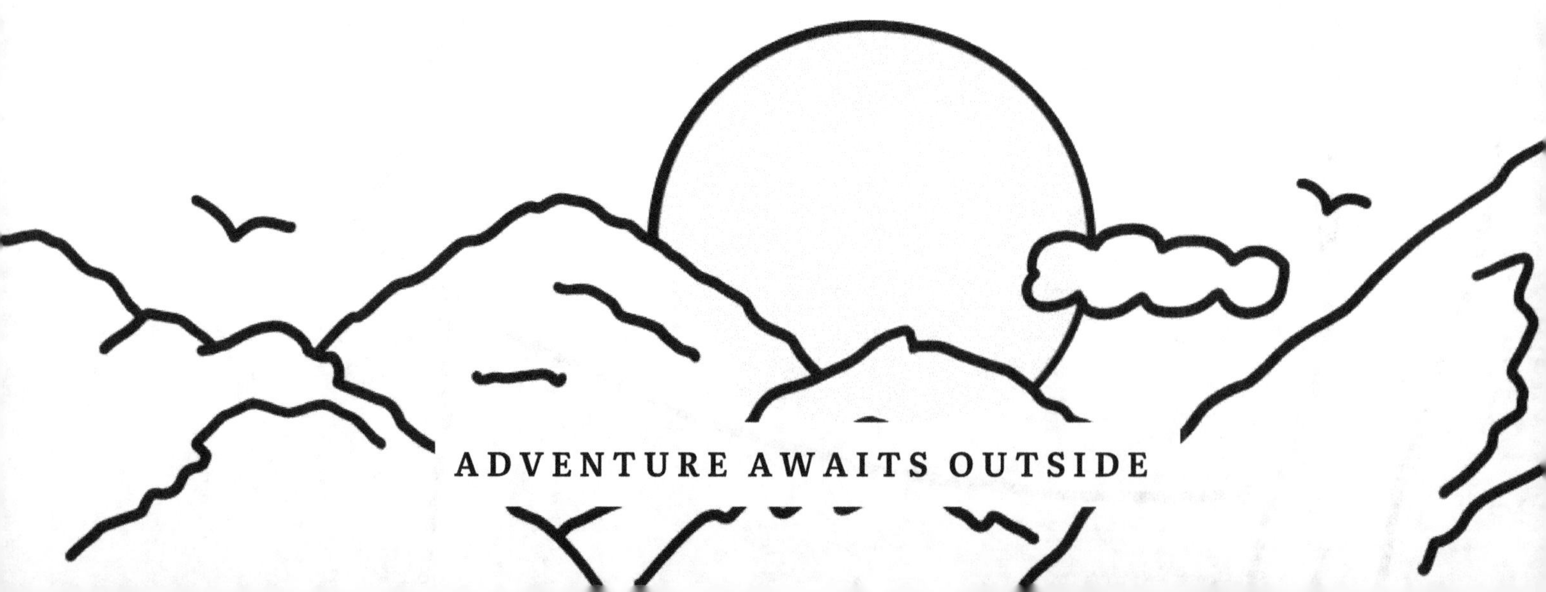

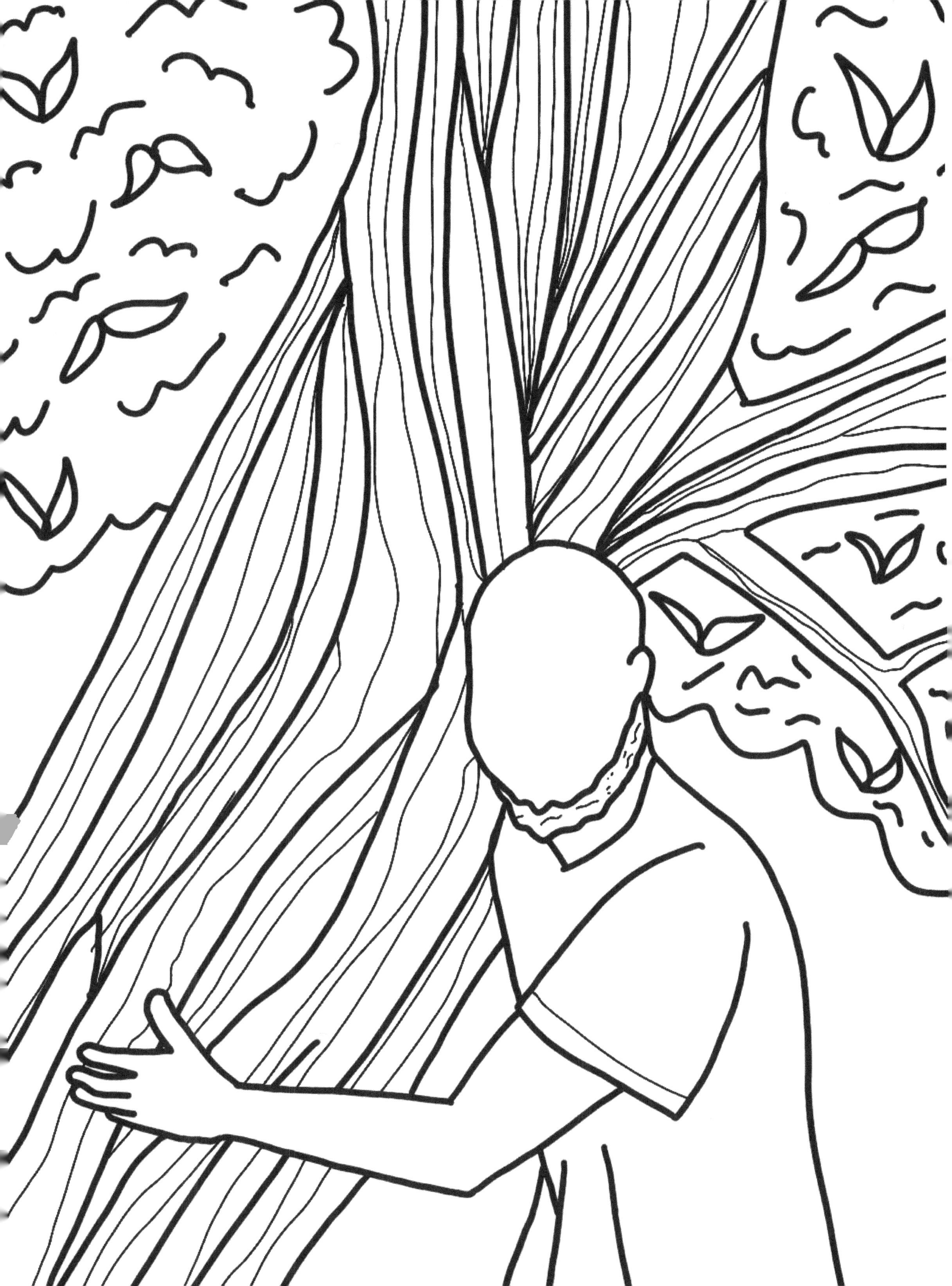

I can do new things.

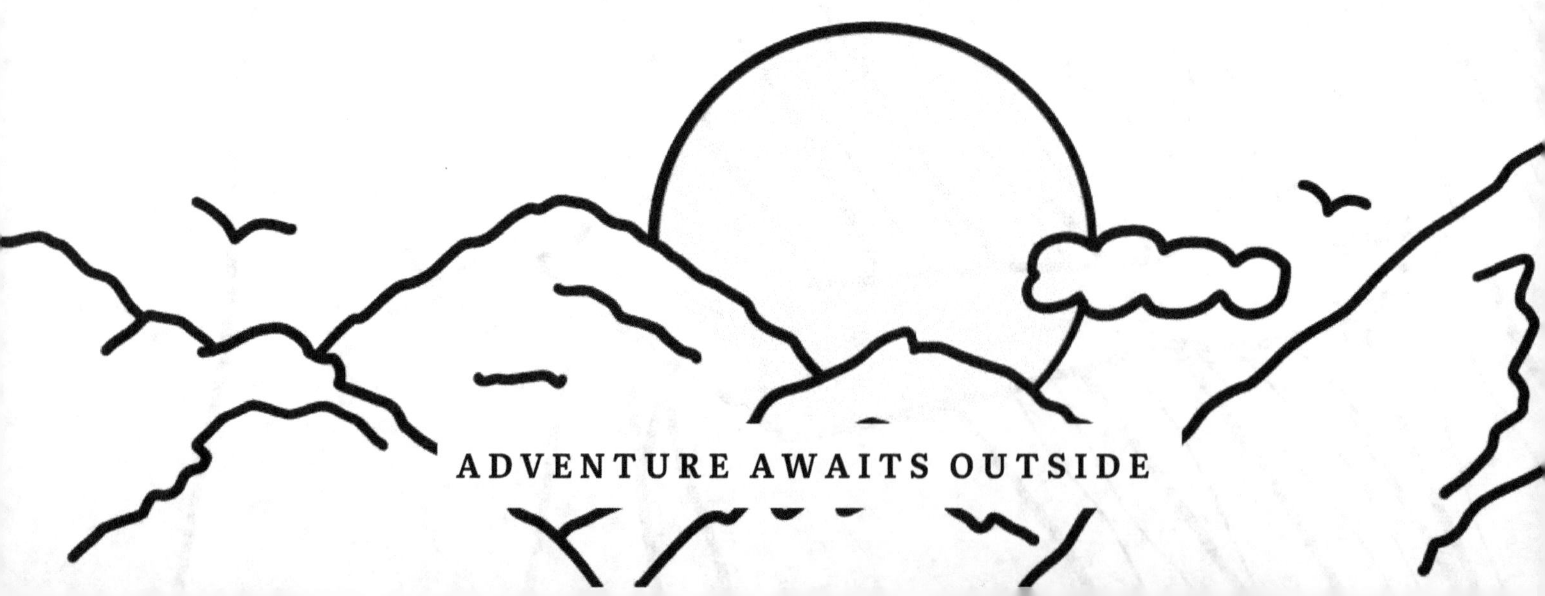

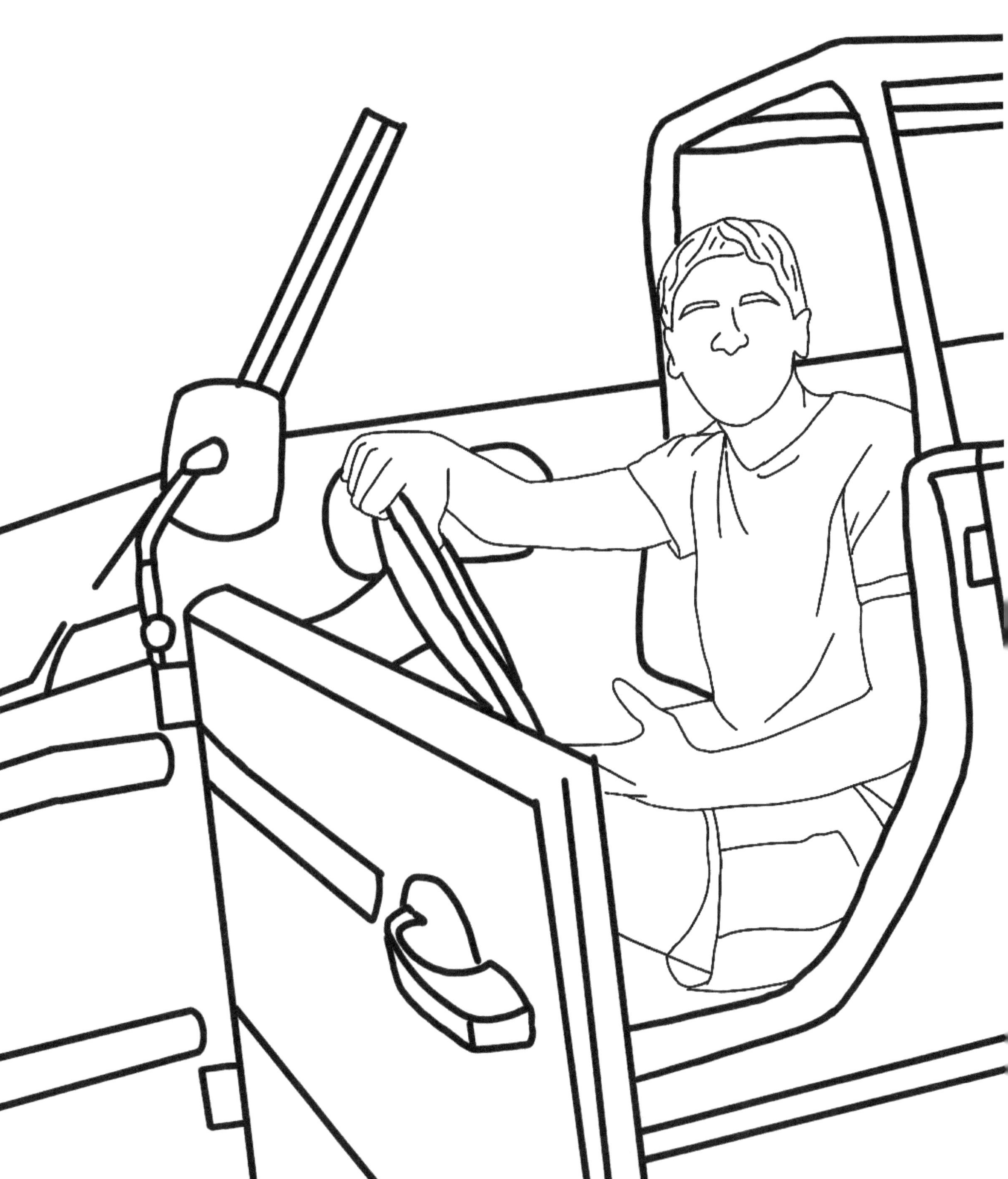

I can do hard things.

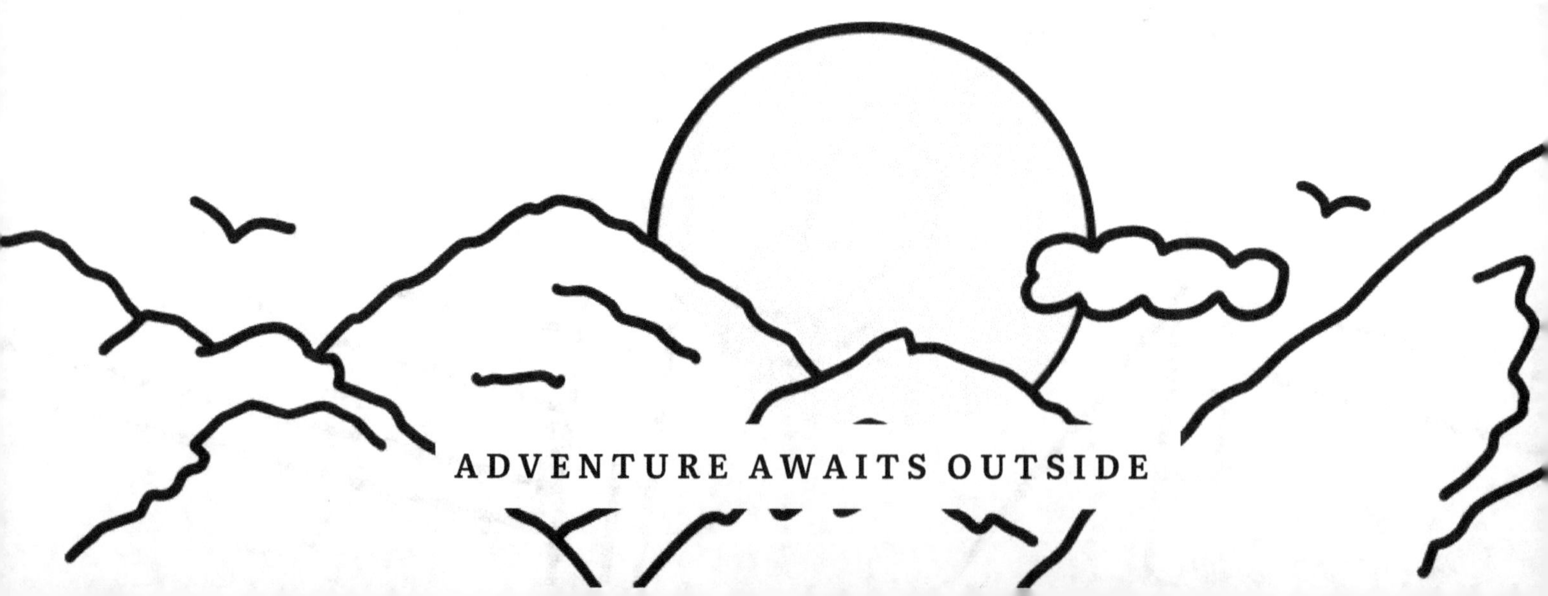

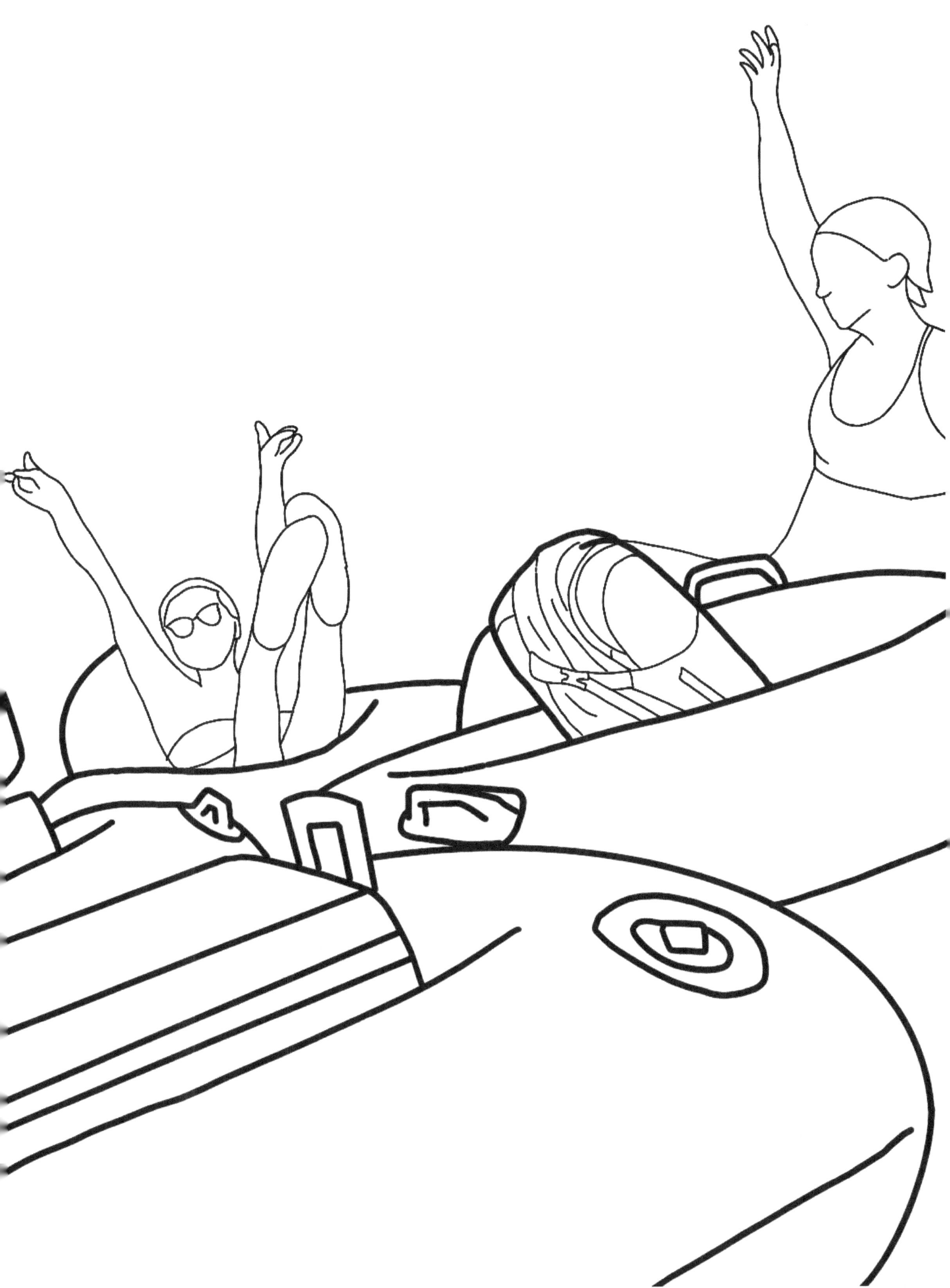

I can get outside of
my comfort zone.

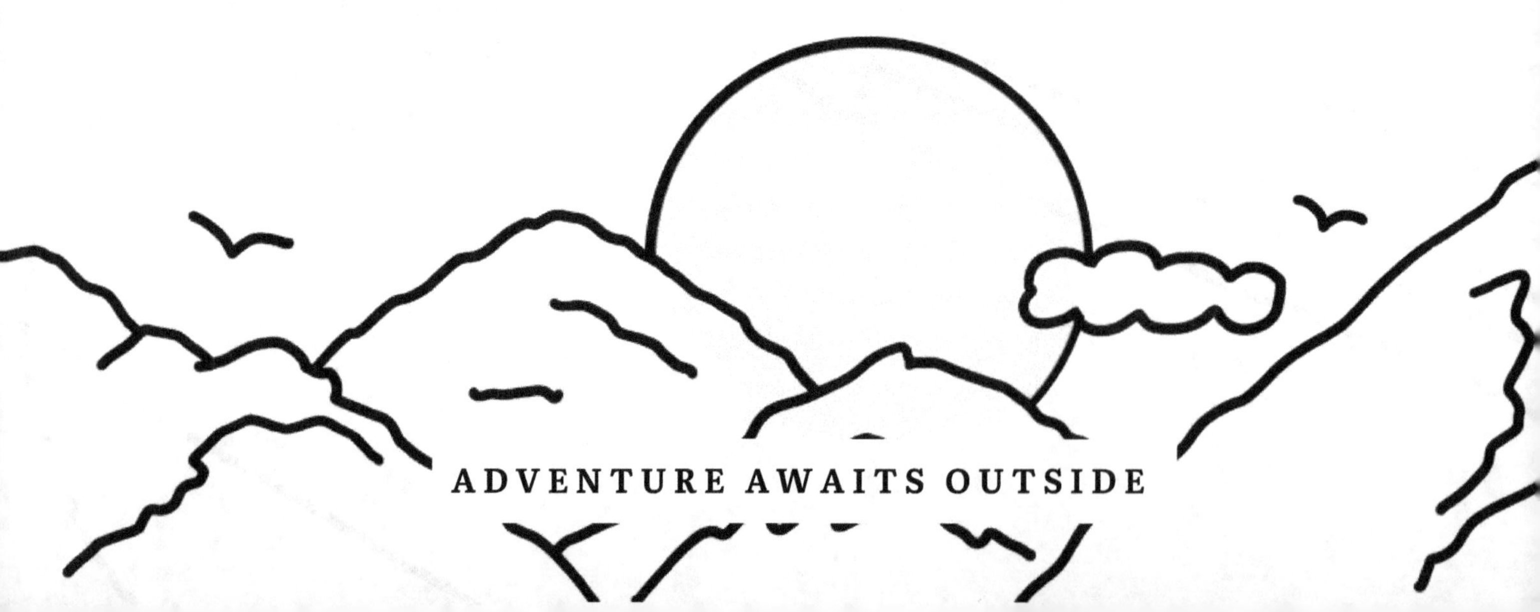

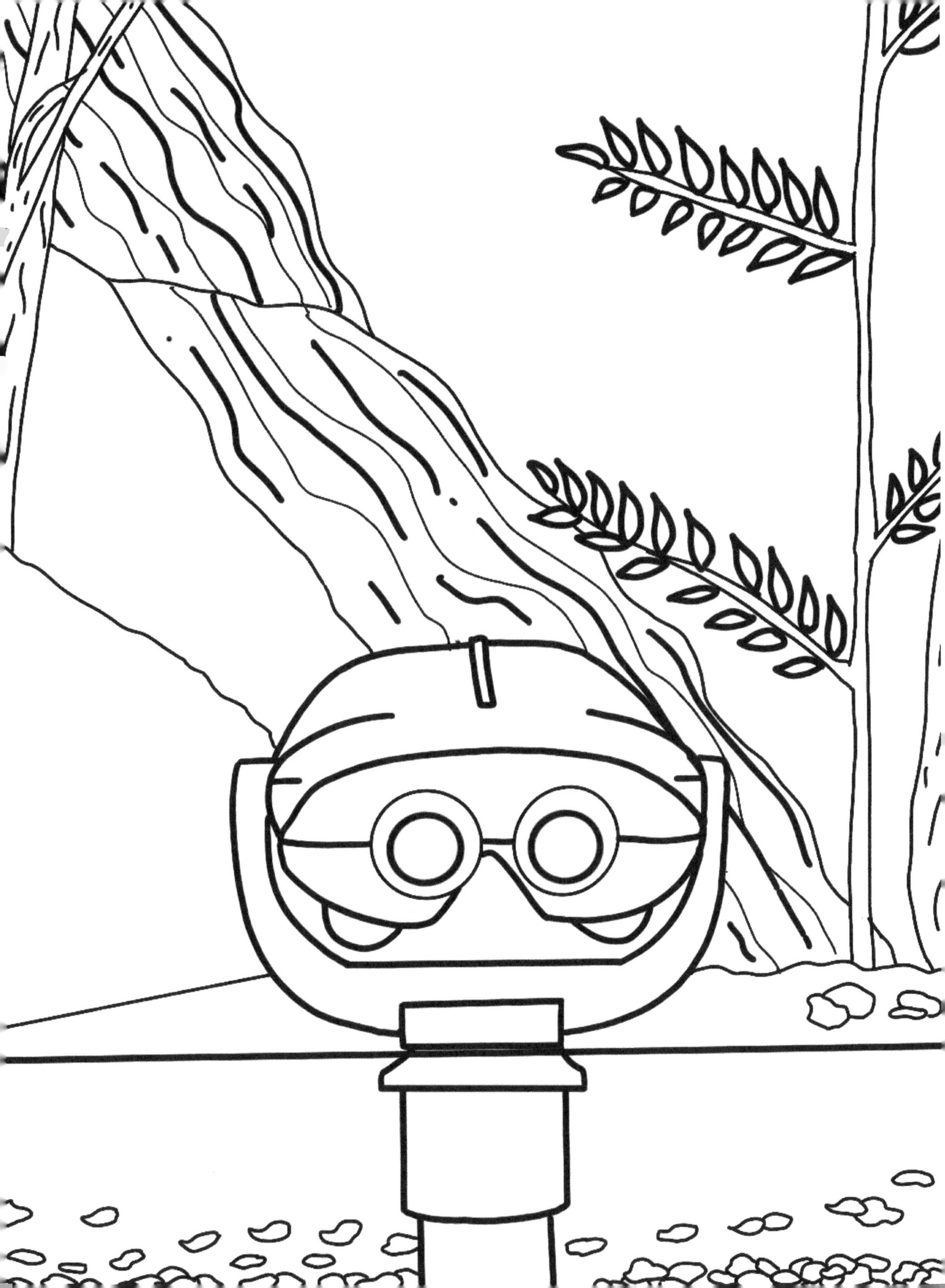

I believe that I can do anything I set my mind to.

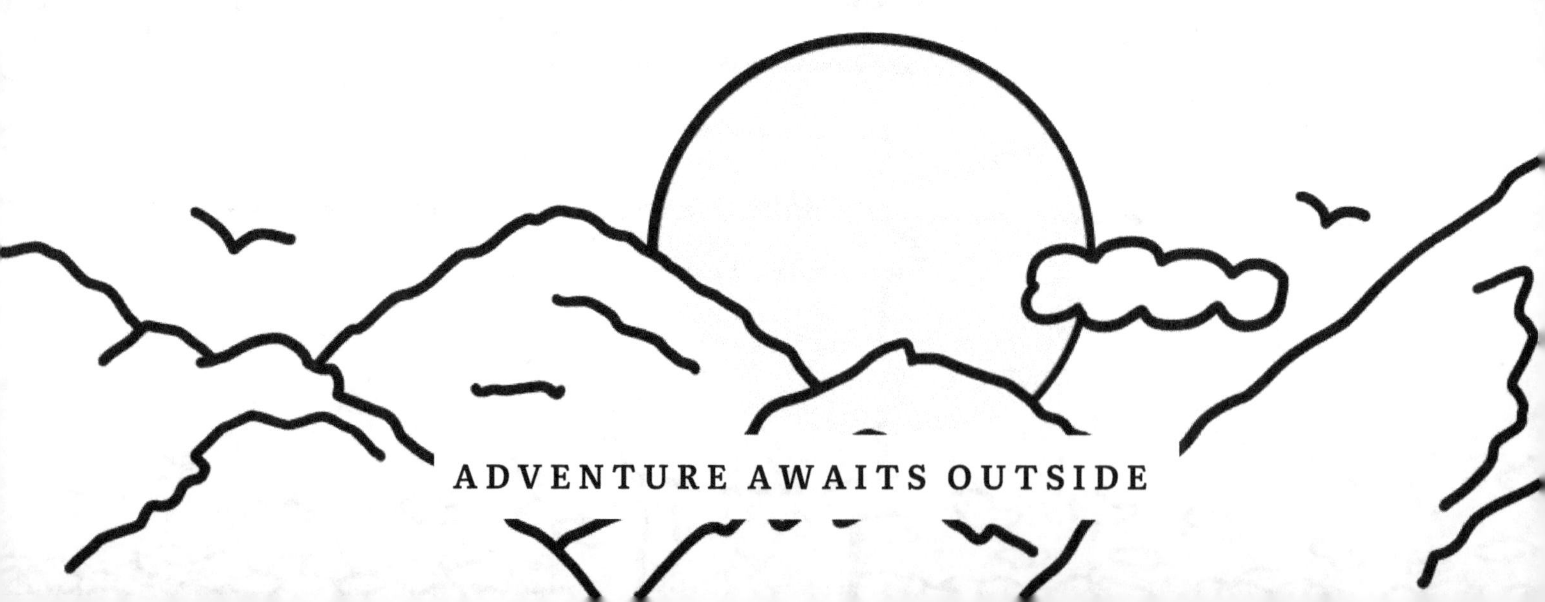

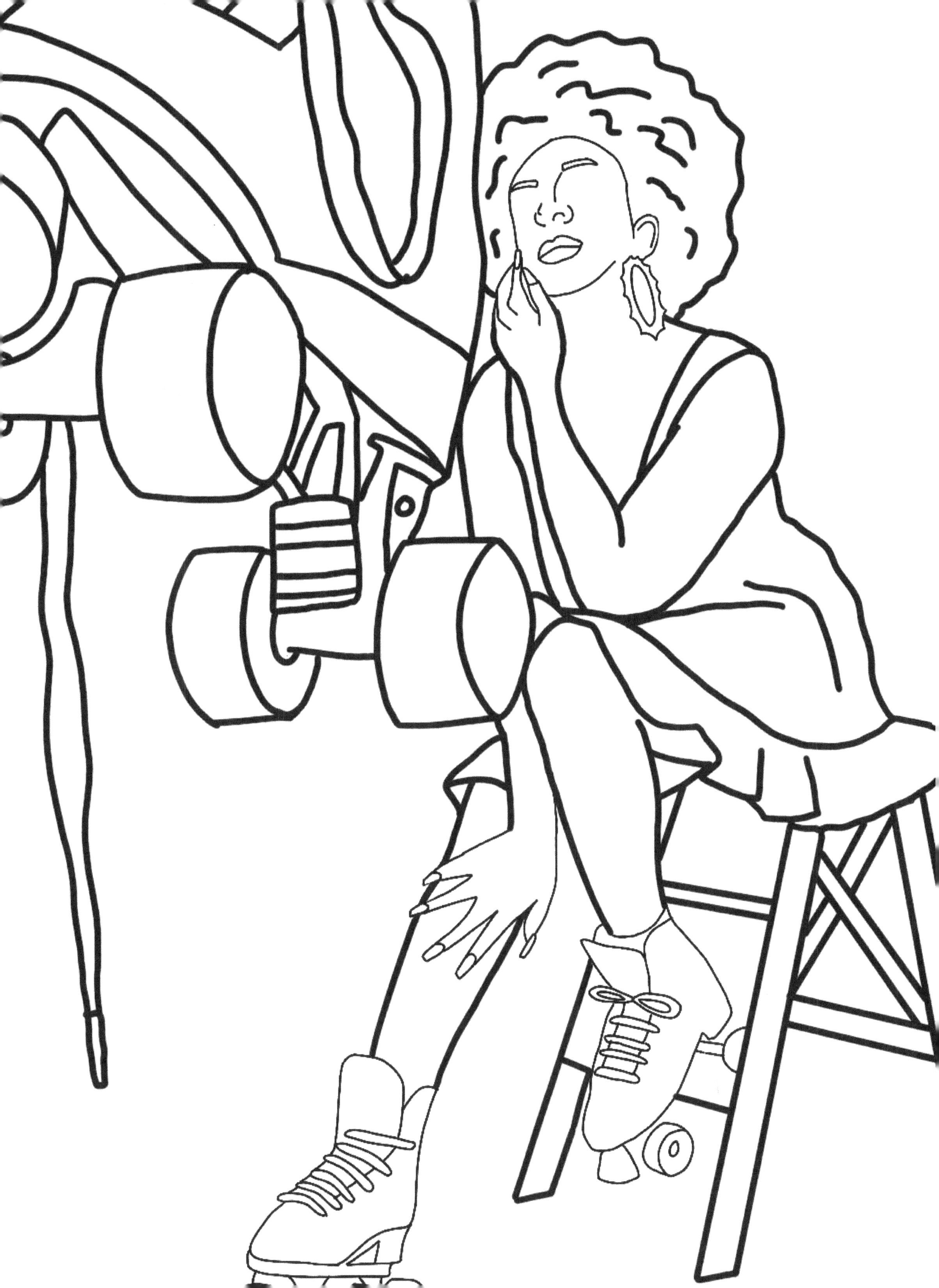

I will learn how to take a calculated risk.

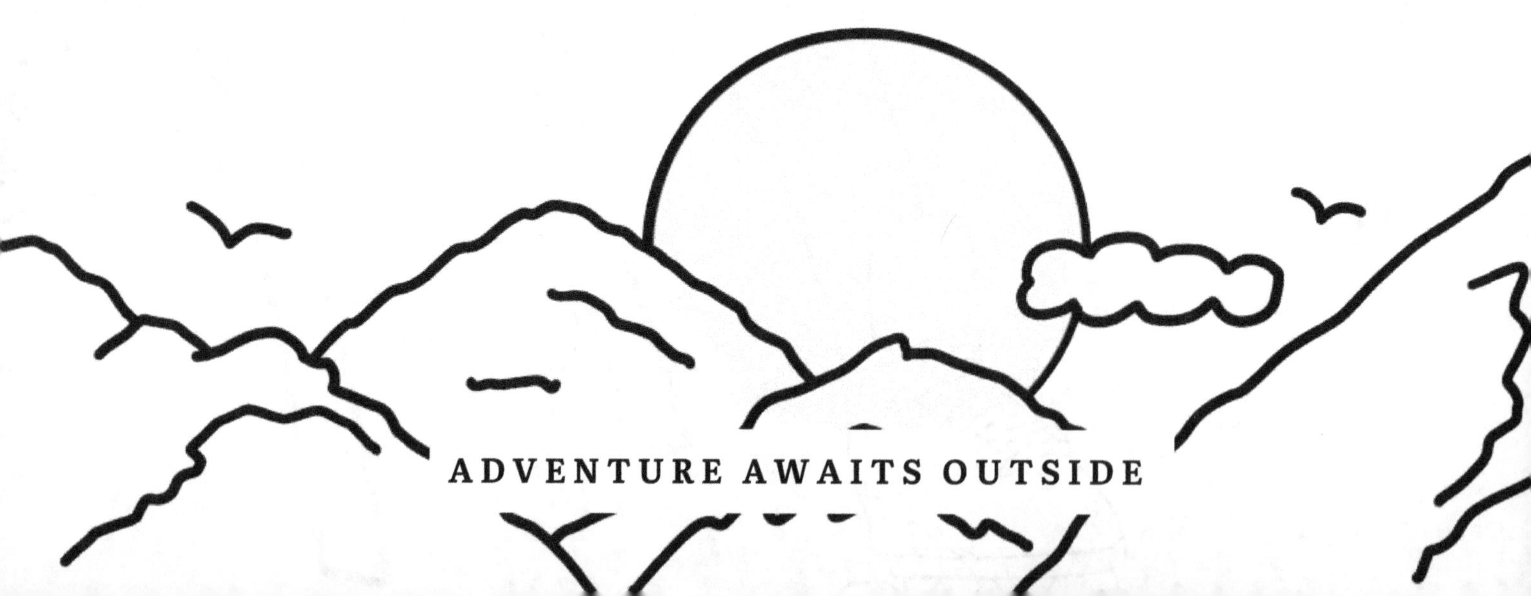

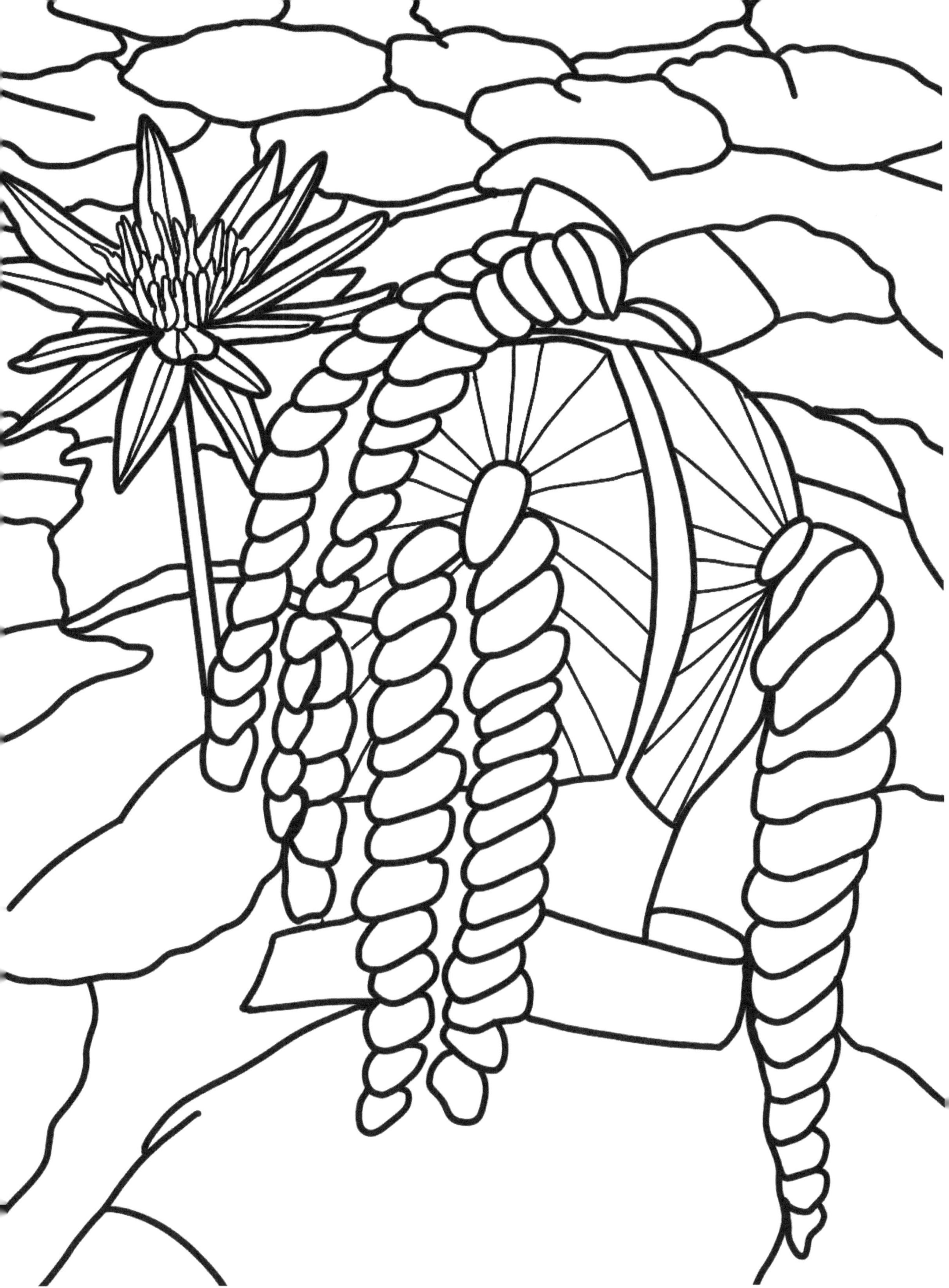

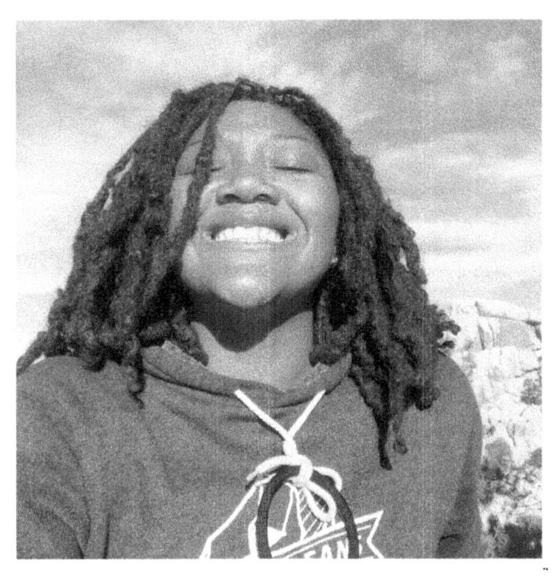

Creative Representation as a Movement for Change

Naomi Winston

Trying new things is scary, without a doubt; even when you are older, it is still scary, but nothing worth gaining is easy. I have gained some of the greatest friends by getting out of my comfort zone because I took the risk to try new things (many of them, and those memories are featured throughout this book).

There are a lot of things in life that are scary, but there is no risk without reward. When you trust yourself to put yourself out there and build the confidence to know that you are amazing no matter what, you will truly be unstoppable.

Always be bold and learn both in and out of the classroom. Try new hobbies, even ones you didn't think you would ever like!

Know that nervousness, fear, and doubt are normal emotions in life but don't let them stop you from working towards the best version of yourself and the people who will join you on that journey.

Remember, everything happens for a reason, and you are everything!